CLOSE TO POWER
A Westminster Life

By

Peter Hill

First published in 2025

Copyright © 2025 Peter Hill

All rights reserved

Published by Peter Hill

Produced by Memoir Magpie www.memoirmagpie.com)

The right of Peter Hill to be identified as the author of this work has been asserted in accordance with Section 77 of the Copyright, Designs and Patents Act 1988. No part of this publication may be copied, reproduced, stored in a retrieval system, or transmitted, in any form or by any means, without the prior permission of Peter Hill, nor be otherwise circulated in any form of binding or cover other than that in which it is published and without a similar condition being imposed on the subsequent purchaser.

ISBN: 978-1-9163777-6-9

Author

The author at 85

Peter Hill comes from North Lincolnshire. He went to school at Christ's Hospital (the Bluecoat School) and won a state scholarship and an Open Exhibition in Classics to Trinity Hall, Cambridge. Before going up he served two years of national service in the Royal Navy, part of it in London at a military section of the School of Slavonic and East European Studies. He learned Russian to interpreter standard. After Cambridge he joined the BBC as a General

Trainee and spent nearly all his career at Westminster as a correspondent and presenter of political programmes such as "Yesterday in Parliament." He also continued in the Royal Naval Reserve for 27 years as a Russian interpreter and was awarded the R.D. and clasp.

After early retirement from the BBC staff, he continued translating and interpreting for businessmen, which took him to Moscow, Hong Kong and Hanoi.

Now in genuine retirement, he paints, learns Italian, plays bridge, and is a National Trust room guide at Petworth House in Sussex.

Also published by Peter Hill: *My Russian Odyssey* (2023).

Note to the Reader

Glossary terms are marked with an asterisk when first used. You'll find explanations for these at the back of the book.

Contents

Foreword 1

Chapter One: Among the Premiers 5

Chapter Two: Getting there.................................25

Chapter Three: Joining the BBC...........................39

Chapter Four: Getting around 46

Chapter Five: Mrs O'Grady 55

Chapter Six: Finding a job; covering elections 60

Chapter Seven: To the Commons 65

Chapter Eight: Thatcher in No.10 81

Chapter Nine: Problems with Benn 93

Chapter Ten: Ups and Downs as a Freelance................102

INDEX 123

Glossary...130

Photos and Sources 137

Fines

Foreword

In my life I have met many people, both famous and infamous. I have only been close to a few. But I have had many encounters which were either amusing, important, or downright comical.

Sometimes I have been a witness to history. It was like having a front seat in the stalls. I was in the Press Gallery* for the momentous vote* to join the European Community. I was there when a gas bomb was thrown. I was there when Airey Neave was assassinated. I watched Michael Heseltine grab the Commons mace in a rage – and then had to interview him about it for TV News. I once persuaded Willie Whitelaw and his Permanent Secretary at the Home Office, Sir Brian Cubbon, to be interviewed together about their mutual enjoyment of *"Yes, Minister"*.

There were other times when I was less of a witness – such as when I was in Brighton for the Tory Party conference in 1984, and slept right through the bomb explosion at the Grand which nearly succeeded in wiping out most of Mrs Thatcher's cabinet.

But this memoir is not just my story. It's an account of how political journalism changed, from an era where the newspapers of Fleet Street reigned supreme, with their regional partners, to the era of 24-hour TV and radio news and digital media. And to unreliable social media. It's also about the characters who populated Westminster - the ambitious, the principled, the eccentric, and occasionally the drunk. It's about the battles we fought to bring the workings of Parliament directly into people's homes. And it's about the changing relationship between politicians and the press, for better and sometimes for worse.

The nature of my work for the BBC brought me into contact with many leading politicians. I never kept a diary, so what follows depends on memory, which can sometimes be faulty. But at least it edits out the trivial and retains the memorable. So here is an account of life among the politicians. I've tried to be honest about my mistakes as well as my successes. There were scoops I missed and judgments I got wrong. Like the time I decided not to interview a clearly inebriated former Foreign Secretary, only to watch rival broadcasters lead their bulletins with his dramatic fall from grace.

But there were triumphs too. I was in the studio through election night when Harold Wilson secured his razor-thin majority in 1964, I heard Margaret Thatcher defy the Brighton bombers, and I was involved when Parliament was first broadcast to the nation. I reported from the Press Gallery by storm lantern during power cuts, and briefly through clouds of CS gas after an attack on the Chamber. I interviewed every Prime Minister from Sir Alec Douglas-Home to John Major - with mixed success!

Although I presented a political programme, "Westminster", for four years on BBC-2, I was never a star of TV. I became an expert on elections and covered many campaigns. I regularly covered party conferences, and for decades toured the seaside resorts of Britain for TV and radio. As time went by I became more comfortable as a radio presenter, and following a spell as presenter of *In Committee* on Radio 4 and then of *Yesterday in Parliament*, I found myself among the team setting up the digital *News on Line*, writing fairly robust profiles of MPs, followed by pen portraits of their fellow members of the devolved Scottish, Welsh and Northern Ireland Parliaments, and then of the MEPs who represented Britain in Strasbourg and Brussels.

Looking back, I was privileged to be part of this period of profound change in British political life – Parliament has been transformed, its hours altered, its powers devolved to Scotland Wales and Northern Ireland, its membership of the EU voted on, and then revoked, its use of referenda increased, its proceedings broadcast, first on radio and then on television. The press has retreated from the Commons Gallery like the tide going out on a beach. Reporters watch the Chamber from offices across the road. Technology has been miniaturised, and news is increasingly digital. Relations with politicians haven't changed much: but public accountability has risen.

I hope what I have written underlines the importance of free reporting of Parliament, and its role in a functioning democracy, even when it is uncomfortable for MPs and ministers; voters have a right to know the truth about those they elect.

What follows is not a comprehensive history of post-war British politics. Rather, it's a personal account of what it was like to be there, in the gallery and the corridors, as history unfolded. It also tells of who I met when I was growing up, how I was educated, who I mixed with at university, and how the BBC trained me. In the Lords and the Commons, and during elections, I met a lot of politicians and did countless interviews. Did they go well? Read on…..!

Peter Hill

Petersfield 2025

Chapter One: Among the Premiers

Sir Alec Douglas-Home

My first introduction to a Prime Minister did not go well, setting the tone for later ones.

In the autumn of 1963, I was working as a BBC general trainee on the old "Tonight" programme, which was presented by Cliff Michelmore. The boss of the BBC Current Affairs section at Lime Grove was the formidable Grace Wyndham Goldie. In August of that year the government had an international success, being a signatory, along with President John F. Kennedy, to the limited Nuclear Test Ban Treaty. The then Conservative British Prime Minster was Sir Alec Douglas-Home, a benign and charming man who, I later discovered, liked nothing more than discussing cricket. To celebrate the great event, the PM arrived at Lime Grove studios to be interviewed.

Chapter One: Among the Premiers

Afterwards, a number of people were lined up in Grace's office for drinks and to be introduced. I don't know why I was there, but I was. She moved down the line. "This is Alasdair Milne, the editor.... and Cliff Michelmore, the presenter... Bryan Redhead...Derek Hart ...Kenneth Alsop.. .Fyfe Robertson..... She reached me, the last one in the line. "And who are you?" she asked loudly. Sir Alec still shook hands.

Chapter One: Among the Premiers

John Major

Thirty years later, I had another boss who hadn't done his homework. Samir Shah, who much later became Chairman of the BBC, was head of Parliamentary programmes at the BBC offices on Millbank. As a freelance*, in the early 1990s, with BBC backing, I had prepared and written an exhibition on the history of the reporting of Parliament, centring around the role of Dr Johnson. It was set out in the attic of Dr Johnson's  house in Gough Square, just off Fleet Street. This was where the great Doctor had written his famous Dictionary. The enterprising Lord Harmsworth, who had commissioned the exhibition, cold-called No.10 and asked John Major, the current Prime Minister, if he would care to open it. To our surprise, he said yes, providing we could fit in with his schedule. So one Monday morning a procession of black limousines rolled up outside the house, and the Prime Minister was welcomed and taken down the line of trustees by Lord Harmsworth, and then by Samir Shah down the line of editors, designers and creators. I was standing next to Andrea, the wife of my BBC colleague Bob Eggington. Shah said to the Prime Minister: "This is Peter Hill, who wrote

Chapter One: Among the Premiers

the exhibition… and this is Mrs Hill…" I almost leapt in the air. "No! She's not my wife!" I exclaimed. Major found this very amusing, and gently leaned forward and said in my ear "I almost changed your life there!" and went on down the line. He then asked to be personally guided through the exhibition, and I spent half an hour with him alone. He showed a keen interest in what was displayed.

Chapter One: Among the Premiers

Harold Macmillan

I was born in the year Neville Chamberlain became Prime Minister, but the nearest I got to his successor, Winston Churchill, was walking past his coffin in Westminster Hall at his Lying-in-State.

However, as an undergraduate at Cambridge I had a brush with Harold Macmillan. I had taken the precaution of joining all three political parties when I went up, so when Macmillan was to address the members of C.U.C.A.(the Cambridge University Conservative Association) in the Guildhall, I was able to get in. I was on the staff of 'Varsity', the undergraduate newspaper, so was able to sit at a press table near the front, next to David Frost, who at the time was editor of 'Granta'. Macmillan was staying at the Garden House Hotel and had a friendly gossip at the bar with the leading student Tories in C.U.C.A., Norman Fowler and Peter Temple-Morris, before coming on to the main event. I believe he asked Norman what young people were thinking nowadays, which laid rather a heavy burden on him as the spokesman for a generation! At the press table in the Guildhall, we were issued with

Chapter One: Among the Premiers

handouts of the P.M.'s speech. Part of it was a heart-wrenching flashback to the First World War and to his time in the trenches and to all the young lives lost. I give the gist, rather than his actual words. "For such a thing to happen again is....er...er.." Macmillan stretched out his arm in the air for the word he was looking for. "It is... er ..." Meanwhile Frosty and I were looking at a text where the word 'Inconceivable' was neatly typed up. "It is, er, er.." We almost shouted it out to him. Macmillan knew exactly what he was searching for. "Yes," he said triumphantly, "it is...inconceivable!". And there was a lesson for us in show-biz oratory by the old actor-manager himself.

We went back for a drink in the Eden Room at Trinity Hall, hosted by Norman Fowler. Macmillan was surrounded by a crowd of undergraduates, where the talk turned to Africa, the 'wind of change' and so on. Through the throng around the P.M. emerged an ambitious student Conservative, Nicholas Budgen, later to become a Tory MP. With scant respect for the great man, he regaled him with an account of a trip to South Africa. There was "much mirth" according to one who was there, and the PM ended up "resting a weary arm round Nick's shoulder". I also recall a witty retort at the time by Macmillan, though Norman says it was not in the Eden Room. It was 1960, and there had recently been a famous literary trial. Someone asked him: "Tell me, Prime Minister, have you ever read *Lady Chatterley's Lover*?" "No", he replied imperturbably. "I usually curl up in bed with a Trollope".

Chapter One: Among the Premiers

Harold Wilson

Unlike some Prime Ministers, Wilson was easy to interview. He did not ask for the questions in advance, and he was affable. He was good at remembering names and faces, and perhaps he was friendly because he recalled an earlier encounter, trivial though it was, when I was a trainee on *South at Six* at Southampton in the early Sixties. Wilson,  then Leader of the Opposition, was coming down from London to give a speech. Would he appear first on *South at Six*, live? Yes, he would. To my surprise, I was asked by the editor to go and pick him up from Southampton railway station. I feared he and his entourage might be too large for my small car. But to my further surprise, there he was coming along the platform all by himself, no security guards, no PAs, no Public Relations man from the Press Office. He was wearing his usual Gannex mac. He was very cheerful and talkative. I got him into my Triumph Herald (my first car ever, for which the BBC had given me a loan). As I drove to the studio, with very little time to spare, carrying Her Majesty's Leader of the Opposition, I reflected briefly on

Chapter One: Among the Premiers

what might happen if I had an accident. Fortunately for history, I didn't.

Wilson became Prime Minister by a narrow margin in 1964. He went on to win several more elections in 1966, and 1974. Then unexpectedly, in 1976, he resigned. No-one was quite sure at the time why he had done so. I was phoned at home and told to get to Downing Street as soon as I could to do an interview with Harold for Radio 4 News. There is always a queue for such major events. BBC TV, then ITN, then perhaps Sky News, then Radio 4, then the World Service, then overseas broadcasters… I listened to Wilson answering the same series of questions in the same way for others, and then it was my turn. With the cameras in the room still in place, but silent, I ran through my questions to him, adding only one, which others had omitted "Did your wife lean on you …" which he cheerfully rebutted. Still, all went well, and I got my interview with the PM back to Radio News in Broadcasting House.

Not long afterwards, ITN produced a paperback by Anthony Davis called *"Television – Here is the News"*, a history of ITN's coverage of domestic and international news – and the problems of TV journalism. And there on the cover, in full colour, was me with Harold Wilson! The two of us were surrounded by cameras with the ITN label. I wrote to Anthony Davis to say I was flattered, but I had never in my life worked for ITN. He confessed it was his mistake – he thought I was someone else, an ITN journalist called Donald Cullimore. For me, some unearned celebrity!

Chapter One: Among the Premiers

Chapter One: Among the Premiers

James Callaghan

Wilson's successor at No.10, James Callaghan, belied his reputation as 'Sunny Jim'. After the 1975 referendum, held to ask the people whether we wanted to stay in the Common Market, (which they did, by a two thirds majority), I was sent to the Foreign Office to interview Callaghan, then Foreign Secretary. He said before we started: "I am not going to answer any questions about the Labour Party". But after this result, mending the split in the Cabinet, after Harold  Wilson had allowed dissidents like Tony Benn, Michael Foot and Peter Shore to campaign to get Britain to leave, was the only point of news interest. Callaghan said he wanted to concentrate on future relations with the countries of the European Community. I refused to be cowed, and even though he didn't want to answer, I insisted on putting my questions about the party. He was very grumpy and refused to answer them. But better to hear him refuse on microphone, than not at all.

It called to mind an evening years ago when I was working in radio on *The World Tonight,* a current affairs programme that went out on Radio 4, then the Home Service, at 10 pm.

Chapter One: Among the Premiers

My boss, Peter Hardiman Scott, the BBC's Political Correspondent, arrived to do an interview live with Duncan Sandys, the Tory Minister for Commonwealth Relations in the early 60s. When Sandys arrived, he handed Peter a piece of paper and said, "These are the questions I want you to ask me". Peter looked at them and replied, "I'm sorry, Minister, but these are not the questions I want to ask". Sadly, that was the way some ministers behaved in those days.

Jim Callaghan wasn't so nice to me either at the end of one Labour party conference. As the sceneshifters and riggers were pulling everything down around us, I managed to do a TV interview with him about his view of the previous five days. The interview went well, nothing sensational, perfectly usable. As we stood up and took our mikes off, Callaghan said: "Well, thanks for the love-in!" I hope very few people in the technical crew* heard that. He had expected tougher questions.

Chapter One: Among the Premiers

Edward Heath

Edward Heath was also a difficult man to love, though he did me some favours. When I was chosen as a Parliamentary correspondent at Westminster in 1968, I took over the post of the BBC correspondent Edward Rayner, who was recruited by Heath to be his press officer while he was Leader of the Opposition. The Conservative party clearly thought Heath needed a more people- and press-friendly image. And Rayner's job was to help him achieve it. So, one lunchtime he invited select members of the Parliamentary lobby to his rooms in Albany, off Piccadilly, for a buffet lunch and drinks. Cold poached salmon was served on silver salvers with regimental inscriptions. We talked about his record collection, and about his splendid piano. During a lull in the conversation, Rayner suggested to Heath that he tell us what happened at the funeral of Harold Holt, which he had attended. Holt, the Australian PM, disappeared, presumed drowned in the ocean. Ted cut Rayner off with a firm No. A chilly silence ensued. (It turned out the story was that Ted had only one security man, whereas the US President Lyndon Johnson went with a crowd of special agents). As we left the flat, and climbed into taxis to return to the Commons, one lobby hack said loudly "Typical of him to serve cold fish!"

But Ted Heath was good to me. I found his manner intimidating, and when he was Prime Minister, towards the end of the fraught February 1974 election, his Press officer gave me a going-over before I even got near the great man in the studio. However, I always believed that Ministers

Chapter One: Among the Premiers

could, and should, handle interviews themselves, and did not have a right to know every question they were to be asked beforehand. A producer in Bristol had advised me once: "Remember the answers you want to get, not the questions you want to put", which makes very good sense, and means you have to listen carefully to what politicians say. Sometimes you have to say, "I'm sorry, but that's not the question I put". Anyway, on the way to interview Heath at Tory headquarters in Smith Square, I heard on my car radio a recording on the PM programme of a speech by the head of the CBI, Campbell Adamson, which was critical of Heath's trade union laws. So, I decided I had to jettison my previous plan, and to ask him only about Adamson and what he had said. I told Heath's Press Officer of the change of subject when I got to Conservative Central Office, and he was annoyed, as their preparatory briefing had to be scrapped. He wanted to know what my questions were now going to be. They went into a huddle and then Heath gave me the interview. He was none too pleased, both with Adamson and with me. But he did it. It may have been uncomfortable, but I am glad I stood my ground, as it was front page news next morning. I got back to TV Centre somewhat down in the dumps after my experience but was cheered up by a friendly colleague who told me, "Well, you got the story!"

Not too long after Heath lost the Tory leadership to Margaret Thatcher, in 1975, I was the presenter of the "*Westminster*" television programme on BBC-2 and discussed with my producer making an approach to Heath. As it happened, I spotted Heath coming towards me in the

Chapter One: Among the Premiers

Ways and Means Corridor at the Commons. So, plucking up courage, I went straight up to him and asked him if he would do a TV interview. "Make me a proposal" he replied. So, we said that if he agreed, we would do a 15–20-minute interview, over half the programme. That suited him. We went round to his house in Belgravia, taking two camera crews (an unusual luxury), and being at home he was fairly relaxed. I was mildly surprised that he swore. Anyway, when the cameras rolled, he came out with (for a TV news programme) pure gold – he said he wasn't going to the Lords, he wouldn't serve under Mrs Thatcher, and he didn't want to go to Washington as Ambassador. He said that her attitude to comprehensive schools was wrong, and so on and so on. What Ted had said would certainly make big news. I spoke to one or two lobby correspondents from the Sunday newspapers and told them it was important. They all agreed to give the programme a good credit. We arranged a despatch rider to get a transcript from TV Centre to Fleet Street on the Saturday night. The following morning it was front page news in the *Sunday Times*, the *Sunday Express*, and several other papers. But only James Margach of the *Sunday Times* gave us a generous credit. When I asked the *Sunday Express* man why he used the contents but didn't attribute the story, when I had gone so far to help him, he said "it's not the paper's policy to give credits". Not what he said beforehand. I got some credit myself for the interview, but I know I was lucky; I had asked Heath at the right time, when he wanted to make his position public and was given the space to do so.

Chapter One: Among the Premiers

A few years later we had a hilarious encounter at the London Zoo. Heath's PA suggested to me that *Westminster* might like to do something to celebrate Heath's birthday (was it his 60th?). We hit upon the idea of getting him to go to the Zoo to feed one of the two pandas which he had been presented with during a visit to China in 1974. (I cannot remember if it was Ching-Ching or Chia-Chia, but then they do tend to look alike!)

However, although this was meant to be a friendly, almost non-political piece, Heath was not in a co-operative mood. He turned up, but he would not face me, or the camera; and as he stuffed bamboo shoots through the grill of the inner cage to his charming (presumably pre-starved) panda, I put

Chapter One: Among the Premiers

a few friendly questions over Heath's shoulder. He resolutely refused to turn round. "Do you think he recognises you?" I asked, driven to desperation. The shoulders shook a little with mirth. But he wasn't giving much. It is the only interview I ever did with a politician from behind. After he had gone, the cameraman got down to panda level and took some very attractive shots of the rare little beast, chewing contentedly, in contrast to the prickly political big beast I had tried to film*. On the way home the cameraman said from the back of the minivan, "Hey Pete, you missed a trick there". "Why?" "You didn't ask him the killer question." "What was that?" "Mr Heath, do you have the same trouble mating as your panda?"

Chapter One: Among the Premiers

Margaret Thatcher

I had few personal encounters with his successor. But I was in at the beginning. The day in 1975 when Mrs Thatcher was elected by Tory MPs, on the second ballot, to replace Edward Heath, I was there in the Committee corridor when it took place, and we piled into the committee room, much to the annoyance of the Sergeant-at-Arms, with our cameras and microphones, to capture the moment. She was the first woman to lead the party. She stood on the Clerks' table, I recall, in her triumph. I interviewed her for Radio 4 and the PM programme, and to my surprise and pleasure, I recently heard the interview on the 50th anniversary of the event on 11th February 2025 – so the tape must have been preserved in the archives permanently.

From the Press Gallery I reported many of Mrs Thatcher's speeches, including those during the Falklands conflict, the statement unmasking Sir Anthony Blunt as a spy, and her

Chapter One: Among the Premiers

very last, very defiant speech in 1990. I had little to do with her personally, but like most Prime Ministers she always sent me a Christmas card, (so did Wilson and Heath) and she always invited me and my wife Rosemary to her drinks parties for the Lobby* in Downing Street. These were very jolly. On one occasion the drinks appeared to have run out, but she went over to the window and produced a bottle of gin from behind the curtain, which she had secreted there for just this sort of crisis. When one arrived at No.10, she grasped your hand not so much in a handshake as a sort of pull-in, telling you to find a drink, and in one case, who to talk to. "Go and find Quintin", she once said to me and Rosemary, when we were amongst the first arrivals. We moved through into the White Drawing Room. There, alone on a sofa, sat the Lord Chancellor, Lord Hailsham. We tried to engage him in conversation. It wasn't easy. As we conversed, another lobby journalist, not known for his sobriety, staggered into the room carrying a drink. He caught one foot under the edge of an expensive Chinese carpet and fell with a loud bang onto the carpet, throwing his drink all over it, right in front of his Lordship. One of the man's fingers was dislocated and sticking up at an unexpected angle. The flow of Hailsham's speech scarcely ceased, nor did he seem concerned; it was almost as if he expected this sort of behaviour from journalists! Meanwhile we helped the poor chap up, and others came in to escort him away.

Later I recall standing in a group around Denis Thatcher who was complaining that his wife had imposed pay restraint on herself and members of the government for

Chapter One: Among the Premiers

another year – and how was he supposed to live on a salary like that! Was he serious? It was brave of him, because I recall a few years before that a government press officer, Derek Howe, told me that his job was to keep Denis Thatcher out of the news, rather than get him into it.

In October 1984 I was one of the BBC team covering the Tory party conference in Brighton. A bomb, planted by the IRA, went off in the Grand Hotel, on the front, nearly killing the Prime Minister and her husband, but killing five others and cruelly injuring Norman Tebbitt and his wife. I and my colleagues in the BBC had been given rooms in the Royal Albion, a hotel which was quite a walk along the front, and we slept through the explosion. By a piece of good fortune, one fellow-correspondent whom I liked and admired, John Harrison, had been filming a piece for the morning bulletins, and was relaxing with his crew in the Metropole next door to the Grand. The ITV crew had filmed their piece, packed up, and gone back to London. So when the explosion occurred, John and his team were on the spot with their camera and made a moving, and exclusive report on those terrible events, the cabinet ministers in their dressing gowns, the collapsed masonry, and the brave rescues by the emergency services. Meanwhile John Cole secured an interview at the local police station with a defiant Prime Minister, who insisted the conference had to go on, and to start on time, despite everything.

Chapter One: Among the Premiers

Parliamentary Lobby Centenary Lunch, Savoy Hotel, Wd. 18th Jan 1984
Benard Ingham; John Desborough; Sgt-at-Arms; Mrs Thatcher; Speaker, Peter Hill

Chapter Two: Getting there

A wartime childhood

You may wonder how I found myself in a job that involved mixing with Prime Ministers. My early life had scarcely fitted me for the roles I was to play. I grew up in Scunthorpe, in North Lincolnshire, during the war. This was not exciting, at least until the street party to celebrate Victory in Europe (VE Day). Occasionally we would hear the drone of bombers in formation, but it was hard to know whether they were German, on their way to bomb Leeds or Bradford or Liverpool, or RAF planes from the numerous airfields in Lincolnshire. Often at night the big Scunthorpe steelworks sent up an eerie orange glow below the clouds, as slag was being tipped; but curiously the town and the works were not bombed. One theory was that Hitler believed his invasion would succeed, and he needed the steelworks to build more tanks and armaments.

So I and my two brothers went to the local primary schools, unaccompanied, without too much concern. In line with the slogan "Dig for Victory!" my father had an allotment for fresh vegetables and kept hens (eggs could be used for barter); in this way we could have a healthy diet, unrestricted by the food rationing. He was once very shaken when he felt he had to give a lift to the local food inspector, and he had in the boot of his car a side of ham which a local farmer had

Chapter Two: Getting there

given to him. Fortunately, the smell of petrol in his Austin Seven concealed the smell of the meat! Now and then we ate in the British Restaurant, where there was a fixed price meal. And for a treat my father would take us to watch the wrestling in the Baths Hall, which was very entertaining. Or occasionally, to the Old Show Ground to watch Scunthorpe United – rather less entertaining!

Nonetheless, even then I did come across, briefly, some famous figures. Big names would occasionally pass through the town. I recall being taken to meet Jimmy Wilde, a former world champion flyweight boxer, who showed off his Lonsdale Belt. I remember being ushered once into the presence of Len Hutton, probably then the most famous English cricketer, and a Yorkshireman to boot. His skin was nut brown.

Another cricketer who caused more of a stir was the young Fred Trueman. My father was manager of the local Trustee Savings Bank, so was asked to be volunteer treasurer for a number of bodies. He was treasurer of the Lincolnshire County Cricket Club (a minor county) which organised a celebrity match once a year on the ground which was sited at the bottom of our garden. Among the celebrities in one match in 1952 were several West Indian test team players, like Frank Worrell, and there was Fred Trueman, England's ace new fast bowler, who was then doing his National Service in the RAF, at the nearby RAF station of Hemswell. (He was also at this time playing football for Lincoln City). Fred got into a sulk when my father tried to pay him his fee. "I want what Worrell's getting" he said, and rejected the

Chapter Two: Getting there

small brown envelope offered. And when the match started, he insulted the spectators by bowling left arm spin instead of right-arm fast. That evening at a dinner one speaker joked that he didn't understand how few wickets this England bowler had taken, compared with the large number taken by a local Lincolnshire medium-pacer. Fred stood up. "Give us a bloody wicket to bowl on, and I'll bowl on it!", he replied. After the dinner my father saw his chance. Fred was standing in a group with his station commander from Hemswell. He quickly went up and said: "Here is the match fee, Mr Trueman, which the Group Captain and I have agreed", and then beat a hasty retreat. Fred had to take it. All this was recounted to me by my father: a few years later I had my own exchanges with Fred.

During the war my father worked hard to promote National Savings. And this brought an unusual guest to our house in Scunthorpe: George Woodcock, then assistant General Secretary of the TUC. My father, as manager of the Trustee Savings Bank, had organised a meeting at which Woodcock was to give a talk about the importance of savings. He was famous for his bushy eyebrows, his

sharp intelligence and his gruff voice. He stayed in our home overnight and charmed us all by describing his love of cooking, and told us how to prepare his favourite dish, mussels in a cream sauce.

Early Politics

As I got into my teens, I became interested in politics and began to help the local Labour MP at election time. He was a barrister, called Lance Mallalieu, who had been a Liberal in the 1930s, lost his seat and joined the Labour Party, getting himself elected for Brigg (the constituency that at the time included Scunthorpe) in a by-election* in 1948. Both his father and brother were also MPs. He rose eventually to be Deputy Speaker in the House of Commons and was knighted. My role when I went out with him was to knock on the doors in the streets that he was visiting and tell those who were in that they could come and speak to their MP about their problems. We went round several Lincolnshire villages, and I enjoyed meeting the people and seeing Mallalieu at work. He remained a good family friend and entertained me to a meal when my work first took me to the Commons.

Christ's Hospital

When I was eleven, I took the train to Doncaster (one change), the train to King's Cross, the tube to Victoria (two changes), and the train to Christ's Hospital, just south of Horsham. The school had a dedicated train and its own railway station. And for the next eight years I travelled to and fro in my uniform of Tudor gown, knee breeches,

Chapter Two: Getting there

yellow stockings and white 'bands'. This occasionally caused hilarity among soldiers returning to Catterick Camp. "Blimey, mate, when you come in I thought you was a nun!" was one response. Another I recall was "Hey, lad, where's the bottom half of your trousers?" Once someone, probably under the illusion that I was a trainee priest, pressed half-a-crown into my palm in the street. It is worth pointing out that politics did not feature in the curriculum. Nor, from my point of view, did science. I recall studying the history of enclosures in the Eighteenth Century, and the growth of heavy industry in the Nineteenth Century; that was as near as I got. Otherwise, it was Latin prose, Latin verse, Greek prose, Greek verse… I knew more about life in ancient Athens than I did about life at Westminster.

One or two people at the school were to achieve national reputations. One master, W.P.C. 'Beaky' Davies, played rugby for England, at outside centre. One boy, slightly younger than me, was John Snow, who grew up to be a fast bowler in the England test team. A good friend who read Classics with me, Jasper Griffin, achieved a different kind of fame as Public Orator at Oxford University, where he was Classics tutor at Balliol. And we occasionally had distinguished visitors at the school: John Betjeman came to talk about poetry, and I remember him saying how easy it was to write poetry in the style of Longfellow. To prove it he burst into an impromptu versification:

"Here I stand upon the platform

With a sea of faces round me.

Chapter Two: Getting there

Writ up there I see 'Australia'.

Over there I see 'New Zealand'....."

And since we were meeting in the Dominions Library, he managed to weave a good few other names of far-off countries named in the wall inscriptions into his instant verse.

Perhaps our most famous visitor was Field Marshal Lord Montgomery, who came to inspect the school cadet corps. He told us all to get a haircut and awarded a half day's holiday all round. A year or two later I was captain of the school cricket team, and we went to play against St John's, Leatherhead, a public school a few miles away from Horsham. When we went in for lunch, to my surprise, Monty was in the chair. It turned out that from 1950 he had been chairman of the governors of the school. He talked all the time, mainly about himself, with his soft rhotacism ('was I *w*eally *w*ight...?'), and at the end said, "I'll tell you what! I will present a c*w*icket bat to anyone today who scores 50". He should have done his homework. At lunch their team was somewhere around 96 for no wicket, and within a few minutes after lunch he had to find <u>two </u>cricket bats!

Royal Navy Russian

After school I had to go straight into the Royal Navy. Conscription* for boys lasted throughout the 1950s. I learned Russian for two years in London and Scotland, making many friends among my contemporaries. Some are friends to this day. My teachers were Russians, Poles, Serbs, refugees from the Baltic states, former Tsarist officers, and even a few Counts. It was the time of the Cold War, the Russian invasion of Hungary, and the Suez crisis, and we prepared for events which, mercifully, never happened. I had to sign the Official Secrets Act. I don't think the fortnight I spent learning about how to be an interrogator had any effect on my subsequent career as a political journalist! Except, as always: Do your homework. But the interlude was highly academic – after all, a year of my time was at a branch of the School of Slavonic Studies in London University – so the transition to Cambridge was not difficult. Perhaps it meant that after the military discipline of the Joint Service School for Linguists, I was less inclined to work as hard at the Classics as I should have done.

Cambridge Years

Cambridge University offered too many rival temptations. There was the theatre, where Derek Jacobi and Ian McKellen were stars; there was the Footlights Club, where David Frost and Peter Cook shone brightly; there were the politics of the parties and the Cambridge Union, where the

Chapter Two: Getting there

list of future MPs was long: Norman Fowler, Leon Brittan, Norman Lamont, Kenneth Clarke, John Gummer, Michael Howard, Peter Viggers… they became known as 'the Cambridge mafia' . All Conservative. Norman and Peter were in my college and became lifelong friends. And sometimes in my job, years later, I had to interview Leon, whether as a treasury minister or a European Commissioner; he could not have been more helpful. He even once tried to date my girlfriend, though I didn't hold that against him!

A strange encounter occurred when one of my Conservative political friends became chairman of the Conservative students and invited Sir Oswald Mosley to come to Cambridge and speak at the Union. This caused some controversy, and during Mosley's speech a bearded student stood up and threw a jelly at him. His aim was accurate, but he had placed it in a plastic bag, so it left no mark. Sir Oswald made a pompous remark about how he could handle this outside, as he was no mean performer at fisticuffs. Anyway, my friend invited me back for drinks to

Chapter Two: Getting there

a private room in a college – not Trinity Hall – where I stood in the crowd around Sir Oswald. He was a large man, tall, with a black moustache. I must admit he had a certain aura.

I also, by accident, bumped into Freddie Trueman again. He was playing in a Yorkshire XI against the University at Fenner's. For some reason he came to a drinks party in my college, and for some other reason, I was there too. I saw him talking to a couple of girls and ambled over. At a suitable break in the conversation, I intervened with what seemed a polite but apposite remark. Fred turned on me. "And who the 'ell are you?" he asked. I can't remember my reply.

In the Footlights, a club which put on a termly show of satirical songs and sketches, (which I joined on the strength of a few comic scripts), Peter Cook was unstoppable. Almost every sentence was comical. One day I went round with a script to Peter's rooms in Pembroke and knocked on his door. No answer. I knocked again, rather more loudly. Still no answer. I knocked a third time, this time with considerable force.

Chapter Two: Getting there

Still no answer. So I tried the handle. It opened, so I went in, intending to put my script on his table. There in front of me was Peter, in bed with a naked girl. He sat up angrily and shouted at me "Why don't you knock?!" Still, he didn't hold any grudges. Years later, at the Establishment Club, where the great American comedian Lenny Bruce was performing, he invited me and others to come back to his Battersea flat to meet Lenny.

And David Frost was in the next-door college to mine. He was not only secretary of Footlights but he ran the magazine 'Granta'. Many years after university he invited me to a party at the Chelsea Physic Garden, held to raise money for bowel cancer. David was President of the cancer charity. When my wife and I arrived and we shook his hand, I tried to revive memories of our time together at Cambridge, but he was a little hazy about it, and in order to get on to the next couple in the queue, he turned and introduced me to a tall, thin, hairless, gentleman on his left. "Peter", he said, "do you know Nick Leeson?" "No, I'm afraid not", was the unavoidable answer. What do you say to a man who had just come out of Changi Gaol, after bringing down Barings Bank?

I made a lot of friends at Cambridge, and our paths kept crossing through life. Professors, priests, teachers, scientists, lawyers, politicians, and even a Bishop. I became the secretary of my Alumni year at Trinity Hall, the so-called 'Year Rep', and have kept in touch with everyone who wanted to stay in contact. They told me many fascinating things, especially as we got older. And I had friends from

Chapter Two: Getting there

'Varsity', the university newspaper, which I eventually edited - to the detriment of my studies.

While I was an undergraduate I made two epic journeys.

The first was to Russia with, of all groups, the Cambridge University Conservative Association, led by Nick Bethell, who later became a peer. He spoke Russian, like me. On the trip, which took two or three days by rail through Berlin, East Germany, Poland, and Byelorussia, I met Tom Adams, a charming lawyer from Barbados, with a keen intelligence and a fanatical love of cricket. In his London flat he had a set of *Wisdens*. We stuck together because, firstly his camera was stolen, probably in return for his refusal to join the *Intourist* herd, when we visited places where we were supposed to stay together and hear a lecture. I interpreted for him with the hotel manager, saying the camera disappeared from his room after the cleaners had been in. But they denied all knowledge. And secondly, because one day we just went off on our own to find a courthouse, a venture in which we somehow succeeded. Tom was a

Chapter Two: Getting there

barrister and wanted to observe a Russian court in action. Our presence caused such a stir the case was adjourned for some minutes until we had been questioned by the judge about our presence. I said Tom was a legal observer. The case then continued, and at the end – it was a civil dispute between two neighbours in a housing block – both parties came over to tell us how satisfied they were with Soviet justice. Although I didn't see it myself, a friend told me that during a long railway journey Tom produced a pack of cards and challenged some Russian to play poker. He cleaned them out. And what of his later life? He became Head of the BBC Caribbean Service in Bush House, where we used to meet. And after that, Prime Minister of Barbados for nine years. He died of a heart attack at the early age of 53.

The second trip I took, on my own initiative, was to Israel. When I was 22-23, I had a Jewish girl friend who was studying to become a teacher. She gave me a book by Leon Uris called "Exodus". It was the history of the Jews, the diaspora before World War II, during the war, and afterwards, and the period of the Mandate in Palestine, which was the responsibility of the British government. It was administered by Attlee's Labour government. The book also described the founding of the state of Israel in 1948, and the immediately ensuing war against the Arabs. I decided I wanted to go and see for myself.

I went to the Jewish Agency and asked if I could go. They said I should take the train to Marseilles, where I could join a rather clapped-out boat, the *S.S.Artsa*, once an Italian ferry, which was mainly taking British Jewish students to do summer courses. I found that with the exception of a

Chapter Two: Getting there

Roman Catholic priest I was the only '*goy*'* on board. That made me an unwanted object of interest, and I was required to sit on discussion panels and give my views on various issues, though I was not sure who I was supposed to represent. I learned a little Hebrew on my way to Haifa. When I landed in the port of Haifa, I wanted to go to Tel Aviv. I stopped a man on the sidewalk in the street and asked him in my halting Hebrew language where the bus station was. He, fortunately, replied in English that coincidentally he was also going to Tel Aviv by bus, and he accompanied me there. We chatted a lot in the bus. It turned out that he was an English Jew, who had served during the Mandate in the British Army as an artilleryman. With pleasure we ate together and after that he explained how to find the office of the Jewish Agency in Tel Aviv. We said our farewells.

For two to three weeks I lived and worked in a kibbutz* in the Negev desert, where I helped *kibbutzniki*, who were mostly Argentinians, with the irrigation of carrot fields. On some of these days I, or my companion, would be armed with a pistol. I also discovered some very early pieces of pottery in the ploughed fields. I joined desert expeditions to Beersheba to see the Bedouin camel market, and to Avdat, a ruined ancient city in the desert, of the Nabatean civilization. which dated back to the 4th century B.C.

After this stay I travelled up to Jerusalem. Because I am not Jewish, I stayed at the YMCA hotel*, which the Israelis pronounced IMKA - Christian Association for Youth. But Jerusalem is a big city, and soon in my wanderings I got lost. I decided to ask a passer-by how to find the YMCA. I did –

Chapter Two: Getting there

and the man I stopped was the same man I had met on the street in Haifa! It's hard to believe, but it's true.

He helped me for a second time, and he was very lucky for me, because in the YMCA I met a man, a Hungarian, who invited me to his kibbutz in Tiberias, on the shore of the Sea of Galilee. He was a fisherman, and in the night, he carried me in his boat on the Sea of Galilee. He said he was careful not to get too close to the far side, as the Syrians might shoot at him.

After this I went up the valley to Metullah, near the Lebanese border, and with an introduction I was welcomed at another type of kibbutz, Kfar Giladi, this time mainly inhabited by Russians, who had fled south from their country in previous years and stopped here. So I could speak Russian with them. They had apple orchards, they leased out heavy vehicles, and they had chalets for urban Israelis to hire for a holiday. Upper Galilee is beautiful, but can be a very dangerous place to live today, with heavily armed Hezbollah fighters just the other side of the border. When I was there, I was able to walk across unmolested and unquestioned. I spent most of my days helping to pick apples, and joining in the collective activities typical of kibbutz life. Watching a film on a makeshift screen in the open air at night was one thing I remember. When my time came to an end, I returned to Haifa, took a boat to Piraeus, then a train from Athens through Macedonia and Yugoslavia to Munich, and then, as I was running out of money, I hitch-hiked the rest of the way up: Stuttgart, Mainz, Bonn, Aachen, Ghent, Bruges, Ostend and the ferry home. On the last leg I learned not to speak French in Flanders!

Chapter Three: Joining the BBC

The Application Process

What was I going to do with the rest of my life? I started doing the rounds. I took the Foreign Office 'country house' test, which lasted two days and took place in Savile Row. It was very exacting: written papers, precis writing, interviews, mini-debates, and finally an appearance before a panel of around a dozen people. Very intimidating. I think I failed because I claimed, when asked, to know the difference between the public and the private sector, and which was the best target for British overseas aid. I opted for one, but when I was asked why, I was flummoxed. A good lesson: never pretend to knowledge you don't have. The proper answer, for me, was "Could you explain that in a little more detail, please?" or "I'm afraid that is not something I have ever given much thought to". They didn't offer me one of the top vacancies, but they did suggest I might be interested in something at Cheltenham. That sounded suspiciously like GCHQ, and they were really after my Russian. They said the starting salary would be £750 a year. But I did not fancy that. I was told if I joined, I could take the main F.O. entrance exam again a year later.

I decided that my character erred on the side of indiscretion rather than discretion, so I took the three other possibilities more seriously. They were all in the broadcasting and

Chapter Three: Joining the BBC

reporting media. First, I was interviewed by the boss of Reuters, in his vast office in Fleet Street. He stressed that all my written reports would appear anonymously. He wasn't impressed by me, and I got no offer.

The second was ITV, which had decided to start a graduate trainee scheme similar to the BBC one. They only intended to take one such trainee, in the first instance. They had boiled their finalists down to three, of whom one was me, one was a good Cambridge student theatre director, Derek Goldby (later to become a distinguished international stage director), and the third was David Frost. We were interviewed by Guthrie Moir ("I would remind you that I am also Head of Religion" he said at one point) and by Lord Windlesham, who was head of Associated Rediffusion. After the interviews, and a considerable period in the waiting room, His Lordship's secretary came teetering down the corridor and said "Mr Frost, would you come this way, please?". Hello, Good Evening, and Welcome. The theatre director, Mr Goldby, with admirable timing, waited till they were on their way, and then called out to the secretary "What about our expenses?", thus mildly spoiling Mr Frost's coronation. Frost began as a researcher on "This Week", then moved on to presenting pop music shows. I sometimes wonder - whatever happened to him after that?

My third option – I'm getting round to it - was the BBC. I applied, came to 5 Portland Place, and was interviewed by a kind, bald gentleman called Adam Gordon, quite an intellectual, who asked me at one point about Kant's

Chapter Three: Joining the BBC

Categorical Imperatives. I was supposed to know about these from my Moral Sciences studies at university, though my memory of them was a little hazy. Was he showing off, I wonder, or did he *really* know, and was just testing whether I was bluffing? I think I returned to the BBC Appointments Board, with its waiting rooms and clanking X-ray lifts, and there must have been a final sifting; I was told that of 150, about 20 had survived. I then went before a large panel of serious men who asked a variety of questions. It was a difficult situation to handle. Sitting in the middle of a large semi-circular group of interrogators makes it hard to know where to look. I am convinced that it was the Head of BBC Drama, Martin Esslin, who rooted for me, because a) I had just been to visit Israel as a non-Jew to stay on various *kibbutzim* and b) I had recently been to see the Moscow State Art Theatre performing Chekhov plays in the World Theatre season at the Aldwych. So I could talk about them both with enthusiasm and knowledge.

Chapter Three: Joining the BBC

The BBC then made me an offer of a Graduate Traineeship, at £850 a year. I took it. I found out that they had chosen four of us altogether, of whom two were Melvyn Bragg and Phillip Whitehead. In the end, I was the only one of the General Trainees who made a full career in the BBC: Melvyn, after making some excellent arts documentaries on *Monitor*, with Huw Wheldon, went off to ITV to do the *South Bank Show*, write novels, and chair the Radio 4 programme *In Our Time*. He is now a peer of the realm. Phillip became an ITV producer of current affairs programmes, then a Labour MP, (for Derby South) then an MEP, and was a consumer champion, becoming chairman of *Which?*, the Consumer Association, and Chairman of the Fabian Society. One of his hobbies was collecting 'Spy' cartoons, which I also did, and I framed a good number for him over the years. He was a good friend of mine, and tragically died on New Year's Eve, 2005, at the age of 68.

As it turned out, I was never a manager nor a producer, but a performer (mainly at Westminster) throughout my BBC career – and I never had another employer until I went freelance - so I never rose to the dizzy management heights of many other graduate trainees. Indeed, somewhat late in my career, I complained that I was always being rejected for management posts, and was sent by an enlightened Personnel Officer to Cranfield School of Management for a three-week course. At one board (for Head of the Russian Service, I think), I was asked why I would make a good manager when I had had no experience of management. I replied that I knew what to do, as I had been so badly managed myself. The Personnel Officer on the board later rang me up to tell me I should not have said that. I got the same sort of question on a board chaired by John Tusa (ex-performer), and on another by Peter Woon (ex-performer), who during the interview had both feet up on the table between us. I was once invited to accompany the D-G, Ian Trethowan (ex-performer) to Russia as his interpreter. But making that leap from one career ladder to another eluded me for thirty years. So probably the bosses were right.

General Trainee: Bush House

My period of two years as a General Trainee consisted of moving around parts of the BBC at three-month intervals. I started at Bush House (in Aldwych) in the European English Service under Ian Lang. He took me under his wing and let me watch many programmes being put together, then allowed me to do short interviews, and finally asked me

Chapter Three: Joining the BBC

to compile and present a whole Christmas programme. We explored, among other topics, Christmas hit songs, and Christmas drinks, which led to interviews with Dusty Springfield and Mr Sandeman.

The latter sent a case of white port after the interview, which I was not allowed to keep, nor to drink. I have always remembered a remark of Ian Lang's after he read in my script that London's Regent Street was lit up by illuminated life-size angels. "And how do you know how big an angel is?", he asked me. There was one alarming incident I recall when an interviewee, clearly very nervous and not used to speaking in public, fainted at the microphone during a live transmission; his head hit the table with a slight bump. The presenter managed to keep going until the man in front of him came round and resumed his discourse. That takes presence of mind! Bush House was a most enjoyable place to work, with a great canteen. Outsiders often came in for a low-price lunch. It is said that once there was an announcement on the Tannoy: "Will members of the London School of Economics please leave their tables when they have finished their meals as there are members of the BBC waiting to get in". There was also in Bush House a huge variety of very clever people in other language services.

Chapter Three: Joining the BBC

I have kept up my links with Bush throughout my life, playing cricket and dining with The Bushmen, a club of which I later became chairman and historian. I even re-wrote the club's history. I joined the BBC Club and often went there for a drink after six when my working day ended.

I was also sent on a three-week course (at the Langham, I think, or perhaps Marylebone Road) - an introduction to the BBC, of which the most valuable were the practical lectures about microphones, tape recorders, studios and sound (it was all about radio in 1961) given by a very engaging instructor. A lot of top brass came to talk about their problems. I met many different types on this course, from foreign clergy to regional producers.

Chapter Four: Getting around

Round the departments

Other departments I went to included Light Entertainment (then in Aeolian Hall in Bond Street) – because I had been in the Cambridge Footlights – and a small benefit from my time there was that each week I went up to Camden Town to watch the recordings of "Semprini Serenade" and afterwards had lunch with Semprini himself in an Italian restaurant. I met a lot of showbiz figures.

I spent some months with *The World Tonight*, then called *News at Ten*, under the dominating and somewhat intimidating presence of Steve Bonarjee – where I learned to brief well-known presenters like Robert McKenzie and Erskine Childers, and to offer drinks and sandwiches to visiting politicians. But I also read the cuttings and did my homework.

Chapter Four: Getting around

I also joined Radio Features, under Laurence Gilliam, a wonderful laissez-faire department with many talented producers, themselves poets and writers, who did their thinking in the "George," a local pub popular with producers from the Features Department. Under the watchful eye of John Bridges I produced a pilot programme called *"The Thinly Sliced Toast and Fruit Juice Show"* or TSTFJ, a sort of satirical sketch show, with specially written music. It was presented by Eric Merriman, the successful scriptwriter, who wrote *Beyond Our Ken*. It was intended to be a break from the traditional comedian/written sitcom/two music breaks formula which had its origins in the music halls. But it fell foul of the men further up the management chain, probably on grounds of taste. After the making of it, I managed to organise an audition for the Cambridge Footlights team in the presence of an experienced producer called Douglas Cleverdon. But it was only when *"Beyond the Fringe"* reached the West End stage that public tastes, and the BBC's reaction to them, began to change.

During the rehearsals for my pilot programme, I got into some trouble. We had persuaded the famous BBC announcer, John Snagge, to take part; he was very sporting, as the presenter had, at a certain point in the script, to slap

Chapter Four: Getting around

his face, and then utter the line "Oh dear, I knew we'd hit a snag sooner or later". There was an actor in the cast, who often worked with Benny Hill. He kept asking me for a loan. Just until the end of the week. Then I would be sure to get it back. I was on a trainee's salary and couldn't oblige. To get him out of my hair I foolishly said, "Why don't you ask John Snagge?" Well, he did, the cheque bounced, and the great announcer was not pleased.

In the autumn of 1963, I was sent to the Television Music and Arts department and placed in the care of Humphrey Burton. He was making a documentary to go out on the 50th birthday of the composer Benjamin Britten. This was to be a major programme scheduled for November 22nd, 1963. It was to be fronted by Huw Wheldon, and the London Symphony Orchestra was to play some of Britten's music in the studio. I learned a lot from watching the film editor cutting pictures to the music of the Sea Interludes from *'Peter Grimes'*. I was sent to the Imperial War Museum to find photographs which would go on screen to fit an extract from the *'War Requiem,* Wilfred Owen's poem beginning, "Move him into the sun." Humphrey kindly allowed me, for the first and only time in my life, to direct in the gallery that passage from the work, using the score, and not a script. It was difficult, but I managed it with some helpful guidance. And my other task was to look after the Russian conductor, Gennadi Rozhdestvenskii, as I spoke Russian. This wasn't really necessary, as when I went to his hotel, he spoke to me in pretty good English. The programme was assembled, we were all ready to go, and we recorded it. On Nov. 22nd around 7pm, about an hour before our transmission time,

Chapter Four: Getting around

the news came that President Kennedy had been assassinated in Dallas. The BBC bosses decided it should go out, and it did.

Round the Regions

I also was sent on some very enjoyable trips to TV and radio in the regions. My first was to Newcastle for three months, working on "*Voice of the People*", presented by the talented writer and folk singer Alex Glasgow, where I imbibed Geordie culture, visited the folk clubs, the shipyards, the mining villages, and went out with the great reporter Harold Williamson (most memorably, when he interviewed the most tattooed man in Britain); I also went over to Carlisle for a few weeks to help produce a local satellite programme on Radio Carlisle. This was before the days of local radio stations. I wrote several scripts for them about famous crimes in Cumbria.

Later I was attached to BBC Southampton, in the newsroom of "South at Six", which overlooked the Trans-Atlantic liner terminal. The chief presenter was Martin Muncaster, who later in life I bumped into in my adopted town of Petersfield. I was given a few try-outs on camera in the live programme - and one of them led to the scariest experience I ever had in TV. It was before the days of autocue*. I was supposed to stand in front of a map of the South Region, and on cue, do my piece to camera while pointing out the places affected. However, two things happened, which in retrospect seem simultaneous, but probably weren't. Firstly, I had written out what I had to say on a series of large cue cards which were hung below the camera. However, I had

Chapter Four: Getting around

used a felt-tip marker pen, and the heat of the studio lights dried out my writing and slowly faded it to the near imperceptible. I strained more and more to see my script. But secondly, there were only a couple of cameras in the studio, and one cameraman; and as I was straining to read from one, the cameraman came round to fix the second camera and blocked my view of what I had to say. I just ground to a halt. I couldn't say to the listening public, "I'm sorry but there is a man in the way!" or "Can we just pause for a moment". I wasn't experienced enough to ad-lib in the hope that events would move my way. I just froze. I am told it was about 8-10 seconds, but it seemed a lifetime to me, and to the director in the gallery it was inexplicable. I cannot remember how it was all resolved but I did few live pieces to camera for *South at Six* after that!

One of those I once had to interview live on "Points West" was Enoch Powell. Before going to the studio I took him to the Green Room. He surprised everyone there by asking "Has anybody got a pair of scissors?" A pair was soon produced, and he charmed all present by trimming his moustache in a mirror! Some years later, at a Lobby party, he gave me and my wife, newlyweds, some good and amusing advice on how to stay happily married. He could be fierce, and his

Chapter Four: Getting around

political views were highly controversial, but in person I got on well with him.

I went out with reporters and camera crews to see how it was done on film. I got my break when the TV reporter Roger Mills' transport to Brighton broke down, and I had to do a programme about the newly founded Sussex University myself. Among others, I interviewed the very fetching Jay twins, Helen and Catherine, who were then students at Brighton. I also made a few films for the cricket commentator John Arlott. He lived at Alresford, and in the winter, he came into the studio at Southampton to preview the region's football. He also made short documentaries about the towns in the south, and it was my privileged task to go out with a crew and shoot film to match a script which he had already written. Going to Marlborough was one task I enjoyed. In the evenings when he was there John would reminisce over a sherry and tell funny stories from his diverse past as a policeman, BBC poetry producer and cricket commentator. After he died I went to the auction of his collection of rare books, but I could not

51

Chapter Four: Getting around

afford the price of his first editions, which often had a personal dedication to John himself.

Meet the Stars

I had a couple of brief brushes with showbusiness, an area where I do not naturally belong. The first was when I was in Bristol in 1966, and I discovered that after the annual Miss World competition organised by Eric Morley, the girls usually travelled to Bristol and gave a form of pageant in the Colston Hall. Afterwards the winner came over to the BBC Bristol studios and was interviewed on *'Points West'*. I was fortunate enough to meet the winner, Reita Faria, the first Indian to win the title, a doctor, who went on to prefer medicine to modelling. She married an endocrinologist and raised a family in Dublin. The *Bristol Evening Post* carried a piece about her, saying she was dressed in a fetching *sarong*. The editor sent a message to the journalist who wrote that, saying, "Get it right! In India they wear *saris*". The journalist replied, "I'm *sari* I was *sarong*!"

Chapter Four: Getting around

I also hitched a ride to meet the American film star Jayne Mansfield. She was visiting Europe giving cabaret performances in night clubs, and had been in Ireland, to the displeasure of the Catholic church. When she arrived at the English Customs, she was reputed to have said to the officer, "Do you want to see my chihuahuas?" and flashed open her fur coat to reveal two small dogs, one under each arm. She was travelling with her lawyer, who was very protective of her, but he allowed a BBC interview by Bruce Parker to take place, at the Webbington Country Club in the Mendips. It was at a time when her film career was coming to an end, but her fame, combined with a thirst for publicity, kept her going. In her dressing room she wore an absurdly short skirt, but Bruce managed to avoid being distracted, kept his eyes on her face and got the interview. We then went to the large hall to await her performance. And wait we did. She was late by an hour, till nearly midnight, when she appeared, in a backless dress, which had very little at the front. All I can recall is that she told a few smutty jokes, and at some point, took up a violin and played one of Brahms' Hungarian Dances. Not quite what we were

Chapter Four: Getting around

expecting! Her second husband was Micky Hargitay, a Hungarian bodybuilder who won the title of Mr Universe, and she said that Micky had taught her to play the music. Apparently she also played the piano and could speak up to five languages. Not quite the dumb blonde she wanted us to believe. Still, I don't think Jayne, who liked to paint everything pink, from her house to her poodle, was a very happy person, with a trail of unsatisfactory relationships. Maybe she was confused about who she really was. She left us confused. Not long afterwards, she died tragically early, aged 34, in a road accident in Mississippi.

Chapter Five: Mrs O'Grady

Mrs O'Grady

One day in 1962 in the Southampton newsroom, I read a copy of *'Reveille'* which was running a series on famous British women spies, after a government official in the C.O.I., Barbara Fell, was given two years in gaol for breaches of the Official Secrets Act. She leaked papers to a Yugoslav diplomat. I expected the next famous woman spy in the series to be Mata Hari. But no. It was Mrs Dorothy O'Grady of Sandown. I looked at a drawing of a stout woman in a raincoat, with a dog at her side, cutting some telephone wires with a pair of shears. I thought this looked interesting, and Sandown was not too far away from Southampton – over on the ferry to Ryde, and a short ride on the railway to Sandown station. So I found out where she lived – she was out of gaol by this time – rang her up, and asked if I could come and see her.

Chapter Five: Mrs O'Grady

She said yes, so I went to her house one Sunday with a tape recorder and sat down with her. She was keen to tell her story, and it was an astonishing one.

She had been running a boarding house in Sandown near the beach, in which she gave a daily walk to her dog. When the war started her husband, a fireman, went off to London the help fight fires in the Blitz. The beach at Sandown was closed to the public under Defence Regulations. Mrs O'Grady did not agree and persisted in taking her walks. Some soldiers tried to arrest her, but she gave them a ten shilling note to leave her alone, which they did. Mrs O'Grady hated the police and the authorities and made little drawings of where the defence installations were along the coast at Culver Cliff, marking in pen where troop concentrations were and where guns were situated, down to Shanklin and Ventnor. Eventually she was arrested and ordered to appear before Ryde Magistrates' Court. But she did not turn up; instead she went on the run, and stayed for three weeks under a false name in a boarding house near Totland Bay, over by the Needles, where there were other gun emplacements. She had taken to walking around with swastikas cut out of paper in her hair and lapel, and little German flags. Her landlady in Freshwater went through her room when she was out and discovered these effects and called the police. And Mrs O'Grady found herself charged with a breach of the Treachery Act of 1940, in effect, of treason, after being questioned by an officer from MI5.

After a short conversation with Mrs O'Grady I quickly realised that she could not possibly have been a spy. She had

Chapter Five: Mrs O'Grady

no radio, she could not speak German, she had no contact with anyone who could remotely have been a German agent or contact. Indeed, I doubted her rationality when she complained to me that the breed of dog in the *'Reveille'* picture was wrong. This was a labrador, and her dog was a retriever called Bob. There was something odd about her motivation, but I did not then know what it was. She showed me her visitors' book and feared the *'Reveille'* article would stop people coming to her boarding house any more.

The authorities, however, thought otherwise, and she was brought before the Assizes in Winchester. The trial was held *in camera*. As she told me, she was not permitted to talk with her defence counsel, a KC; she was not allowed to go in the witness box, where she hoped, so she said to me, to declare that it was all a bit of a joke; and it ended with the judge donning a black cap and sentencing her to death, the first woman to receive such a sentence under the new law. She said to me she found this rather funny. The whole thing was a travesty. Mercifully, her appeal was successful, and the Home Secretary commuted the sentence to 14 years in prison, which she mostly served in Holloway and Aylesbury. The prison psychologist found her highly intelligent but mentally disturbed and masochistic. She was released in 1950.

When she came out, she went to the *Sunday Express* and told them it had all been a joke, and she had been innocent all along. I believed her. And I was proved right when 55 years later, in 1995, the papers of the trial were unsealed by the Crown Prosecution Service. Most of the press, including the

Chapter Five: Mrs O'Grady

Times, sadly concluded that she had been a Nazi agent. I went to examine the documents in the CPS office on Ludgate Hill. I was only the second person to do so. I was able to inspect the evidence: the little maps she made, the bottle of pills from her handbag, which were not suicide pills but a harmless remedy for a runny nose. No shears, no codes, no transmitters, no radios. The key to her behaviour lay in the letters (which I found in her file), which she wrote from prison to her solicitor, in which she explained her behaviour. It sprang from her youth in London: adopted, bullied by foster parents, and left to her own devices, she became quite a good forger, served time for stealing clothes, and was arrested more than once by the police for soliciting. She was incensed by the fact that she was kept in custody while her little dog at home starved to death. And she swore revenge on the police. And the reason she fled the Ryde magistrates was nothing to do with spying; it was because she did not want her previous convictions read out in court. She had not told her husband about them, and she feared he would attend the hearing and find out. Slowly, her erratic behaviour, though strange, began to make sense. She was a fantasist, a disturbed woman who sought the limelight, but no more than a nuisance who should have done a short sentence for attempted sabotage and wasting police time. I wrote to the leading academic historian of wartime espionage, and he confirmed to me that the Germans as far as he knew had no known agents in place when war broke out. I also found a chilling letter in the archives from the then Director of Public Prosecutions, saying they shouldn't be too concerned about hanging her just because she was a woman. The authorities were keen to show the Germans

Chapter Five: Mrs O'Grady

that any spy of theirs would be put to death. Which is why I regard the actions of MI5, in the face of what they knew about Mrs O'Grady, as far more reprehensible than hers. At any rate, she lived a long life; radio plays and books were written about her; and she died at 87 in a care home, where she was said to have been polite and appreciative. I cannot emphasise too strongly: Mrs O'Grady was not a spy.

The O'Grady story has stayed with me most of my life and I have frequently lectured about her. I have been surprised, even depressed, by how many articles I have read, after the CPS released the court papers, which were written and published by people who had not read the evidence, or gone into the detail, but just parroted and rejigged inaccurate material passed to them by someone else. Several newspapermen who I contacted told me they were given a story written by an Isle of Wight freelance and told to make it up into a feature. And I have been appalled by people, including an MP, who claimed to have seen the files, but never went to the CPS office. And now, I read, the files have gone missing. In 2010 it transpired that the main National Archives file was no longer available, "misplaced when on loan to government department". A book by Adrian Searle in 2012, 'The Spy Beside the Sea' puts a more balanced view.

Chapter Six: Finding a job; covering elections

I was not in Southampton for long. My interests throughout my time as a General Trainee were looked after by Hallam Tennyson, a very nice man, a great-grandson of the Poet Laureate, and himself a playwright, who later wrote a very odd book, revealing his homosexuality. Shockingly, he was later found murdered in his bed. As the supervisor of BBC Trainees, he would get in touch with me from time to time, I would see him, he would fix up my next attachment*, and presumably he got reports back about my progress from wherever I had been.

He advised me about applying for jobs, and late in '63 I got one as a junior producer in the Overseas English Service under Gerry Mansell, one of the best bosses I ever had, who had assembled a fine team of producers, and who kept everyone busy with a large and varied output of current affairs. I produced many short talks such as *"Commentary"* and longer compilation programmes, including *"The World*

Chapter Six: Finding a job, covering elections

Today" and *"People and Politics"*, with Norman Hunt (later Lord Crowther-Hunt); and I not only became very well-informed about foreign affairs, but met most of the international experts from Fleet Street, the LSE and elsewhere. I produced a number of series, including one with Michael Shanks, called *'The ABC of Economics'*, and another, on *'The Changing Face of Communism'*, with Geoffrey Stern of the LSE. I was in the studio team for the important 1964 General Election and played a part in every succeeding election campaign and results night for nearly thirty years.

Looking back, I was hardly ever bored on any of my attachments; I wasn't there to watch other people work. Fortunately, I was given things to do or found things to do. And on the way I learned to cope with the technology of recorders and studios, as well as how to perform at the microphone. I was always less happy in television, where one was always less in control of one's material, and some people in News, I suspected, didn't like my face. They never said why. And although I was given advice on how to read at the radio microphone - and very good it was too - I was never ever given any guidance on how to perform on television, or how to improve my performance. You just got on with it.

Elections

1964 arrived, and the Tories were out. By a whisker. The General Election in October of that year was the first of many that I covered in the studio, and one of the most exciting. I was working as a producer in Bush House covering the General Election for the General Overseas

Chapter Six: Finding a job, covering elections

(later World) Service. Round the table were Bob Reid, Dr Norman Hunt and John Tusa. I sat at the end of the table feeding in information. No computers – all cards from my box file, and agency tape from Reuters and the Press Association*, and voice feeds* from our correspondents in the marginals. The Tories had been in in power since 1951, and Harold Wilson was set fair to give Sir Alec Douglas-Home a close run. In the middle of the night Anatol Goldberg, the sage of the Russian Service, a balding intellectual with a slight stoop to whom we all deferred, suddenly appeared, and took over the microphone. Khruschev had fallen! A story of worldwide importance was breaking in the middle of our domestic election. So news from marginal constituencies was alternating with reaction to Kremlin politics throughout the night – and, with a short break for sleep, throughout most of the next day, Friday, because of the seats where they did not count their votes till the morning. They were mostly rural, and Scottish, and we were on a knife edge, until the final results came in from Ross, Cromarty, Skye, Argyll and Sutherland. We stayed at the microphone in an increasingly messy studio till it was clear that Labour had won – by a majority of four. Douglas-Home was out, and Harold Wilson went to Downing Street. He increased his majority greatly two years later. We stopped the election broadcast marathon eventually at about 4pm.

I count it as a minor triumph, during another election night broadcast, this time from Broadcasting House, that I managed to complete an entire interview with someone whom I had never heard of, and with no explanation as to

Chapter Six: Finding a job, covering elections

why. It must have been about eight o'clock on the Friday morning when we were all suffering from lack of sleep. I was in the studio at the microphone when the election broadcast director, Ann Sloman, said in my earpiece "Stand by to interview John Barnes". Before I could say "Who?" or give an expressive shrug towards the cubicle, he was put through. I think I said something like, "Well, Mr Barnes, what is your view of what is happening?" and hoped to glean a few clues from his answers. I didn't. However, I managed to get through to the end of the interview without revealing either my ignorance, or his relevance. I learned later that he was a well-known academic who had written books about Baldwin and coalitions in the twenties and thirties (there was a prospect that this particular election might produce a coalition) – if only I had known!

I had one big election night success, in 1987, which came about by a lucky accident. I was lunching in the Press Gallery* canteen at the Commons and was joined by that doyen of lobby correspondents, and frequent broadcaster, Bob Carvel of the London *Evening Standard*. He was angry. He had just come from a planning meeting at Broadcasting House, where they were discussing plans for the forthcoming election night results programme. The producer in charge, who shall be nameless, had been rude to him, and suggested he, one of the most experienced and knowledgeable broadcasters in the business, was not up to it. Bob told me he had stood up, and said "in that case, find someone else. I'm going" and walked out. Later that afternoon at the Commons there was a call for me. It was from John Wilson, the editor of Radio News. "Peter", he

Chapter Six: Finding a job, covering elections

said, "how would you like to be the chief commentator in the studio on election night? We have been discussing it and decided that you with your knowledge would be ideal for the task". I did not let on about my lunchtime conversation. "How very kind", I replied, "I would love to do it". And so I spent the next couple of weeks preparing cards on MPs and candidates, in a standard A-Z box file. Laborious, but well worth it, as on the night I found myself sitting in the studio next to the great David Butler from Oxford University, who was getting his information off a TV screen, fed by his son sitting in another room. I still managed to get my cards out and information ready to put on the air before the computer could do it for him! When it was over, it turned out to be Mrs Thatcher's third election victory.

Chapter Seven: To the Commons

To the Commons

BBC Office

In January 1968, as I have mentioned earlier, one of the BBC's Parliamentary reporters, Edward Rayner, was recruited to be Ted Heath's personal press officer, and I applied for the vacancy and was selected. So I moved back to London and began what was to be a thirty year stint at the Houses of Parliament. I joined a small team. A Labour government under Harold Wilson was in power. And the crises were not long in coming. There were three of us in the Press Gallery at the Commons (out of six) whose role was to report the Chamber – Conrad Voss Bark, Christopher Jones and myself. We usually took it in turns to stay late if Commons business went past midnight – but on one fateful night, March 14th, 1968, when a debate on a guillotine* for the Transport Bill was grinding on, Conrad said "This is tedious stuff. We are not going to get anything from it" and said we should all go home. And so we did. But quite unexpectedly, at 3.20 in the morning, the Chancellor of the Exchequer, Roy Jenkins, turned up. The House adjourned and he made a major statement. The London gold market was to be closed the following day. It was at the request of the US authorities, and central bank governors were due to meet at the weekend. There was no-one there

Chapter Seven: To the Commons

in the Gallery from the BBC. A real disaster for us, from which we learned a bitter lesson.

Jenkins Budget

The following year I had a sort of disaster, but I got away with it, because nobody noticed. However, I have always been conscious of this guilty secret. On April 15th 1969, when Roy Jenkins was Chancellor, I had to do the précis of the Budget, live, at the top of the Six O'Clock Radio News. It is one of the really high-pressure spots, and it meant writing my script in the Press Gallery as I went along, while listening to the Chancellor. But Jenkins went on, and on, and on, and he was getting dangerously close to six o'clock. Most Chancellors keep their prize political and popular announcements till the end, and this Budget was no exception. With about fifteen minutes to go he announced that he was going to make changes to the "reduced rate band" of income tax. I did not understand what this meant, so I decided to ignore it – I had quite enough to pass on already - and leave it to the pundits for later. So I rushed out of the gallery and into the Studio box with its lip mike*, and, trying to sound calm, I gave all the other Budget details, live at the top of the news, from the script I had prepared. Jenkins finally sat down around two minutes to six, after a speech of two and a half hours. It was only later that I discovered that the bit that I left out was in fact an important element in the Budget, if not *the* most important, affecting over a million poor people, who in the future were to pay income tax at a lower rate than the standard rate, because their personal allowances were to be raised. The cost of the

Chapter Seven: To the Commons

changes was £14 million in a full year. However, no-one – not the newsroom editors, nor my colleagues, nor the Treasury press office, - spotted the omission, and I survived. Only now do I confess!

A few weeks earlier I was involved in a confrontation with the extrovert Tory MP Sir Gerald Nabarro, known for his loud voice, handlebar moustaches, and expert knowledge of purchase tax*. It was finally solved by this Budget. In the chamber one day, some weeks previously, he had noisily predicted that the Chancellor was going to increase the car tax, and that he had seen documentary proof of it, supplied by printers. A select committee* was set up by the House to investigate, and reported there had been no Budget leak. But Sir Gerald persisted. I was detailed off to interview him for a news programme around 7.30p.m. on BBC-2. Unfortunately, the interview was to take place in the TV studio in Broadcasting House, which was unmanned and had only one camera. It was normally used for reporters doing straight pieces to camera. I agreed down the line with

Chapter Seven: To the Commons

the director that I would start by doing a live straight piece, reporting what had happened, then he would pull out to a two-shot, where Sir Gerald would be found sitting alongside me for the interview, and he would then close in on the moustachioed one as he gave his answers. I got him in place, but as I did my report, various "harrumphs" could be heard off camera, as he disagreed with my version of events. When I turned and asked him how he could possibly know, when the Treasury was saying the decision hadn't been made, he got rather personal. Instead of giving proper answers to the questions, he attacked me. "Who do you think you are, young man", he bellowed, "the poor man's Robin Day?" I persevered and was later praised for keeping cool. The interview was used elsewhere, including on the later 9 O'Clock news on BBC1. The public could judge. As we left the studio, and he got out of performance mode, he calmly turned to me and said "Well, I've got him over a barrel." (Meaning Jenkins). "If he puts the tax up, I will say, 'I told you so'; if he doesn't, I will say, 'well it was me that stopped it". I left rather red in the face, appalled at his cynicism, but colleagues said to me later, "Great television!"

In the event Roy Jenkins stated in his Budget speech that he had no intention of putting car tax up, and he had noted this in a Treasury minute dated 31st December 1968 – four months previously.

Gas and bombs

Conditions in the Commons have not always been ideal. I have reported from the Press Gallery by storm lantern (when there was a power cut during the miners' strike) and

Chapter Seven: To the Commons

in a cloud of CS gas, after two canisters were thrown into the Chamber from the public gallery by an aggrieved Irishman. As the Tory Minister, Anthony Barber, was making a statement to the House in July 1970, a young man stood in the public gallery, shouted "Belfast! See how you like it!" and threw two CS gas canisters into the chamber below. One rolled near the Despatch Box*. Barbara Castle was nearby. So were Bob Mellish, George Thompson and Fred Peart, who tried to kick the canister away. They beat a speedy retreat. The elderly Speaker, Dr Horace King, was overcome, and was carried out by the former actor and Labour MP Andrew Faulds. Several MPs were badly affected. The Labour MP Tom Swain, an ex-miner, who always sat in the front row of seats, was taken to hospital together with two staff members. Business was suspended for nearly two hours. We were assured that the air-conditioning in the Chamber was efficient. But when the House resumed – and MPs were keen not to let such attacks hold up the conduct of business – it was still very unpleasant. We reporters could only sit in the Gallery for about ten minutes at the most before we came out, weeping.

Whitehall bomb

In March 1973 the Provisional IRA mounted a major bomb attack in London. I played a small part in it all. I was walking back to the office through Parliament Square when I heard an explosion. From the top of Whitehall I could see a cloud of smoke rising, about half way down on the right. I called a cab and said, for the first and only time in my life, "Take me to the explosion!" The cabbie did not demur, with an

Chapter Seven: To the Commons

"OK, Guv, I'll try", and we drove down as far as we could. The police were beginning to tape off the area. On the pavement, to my surprise, the first person I saw, and recognised, was the Duke of Kent, legging it away from the scene of the crime. It was clear the bomb had gone off in a side street next to an Army Recruiting Centre, and New Scotland Yard. I learned later that the authorities had had some advance warning of the car bombs and had defused one outside Scotland Yard. I recall the time was about twenty to three and I immediately felt that I should phone through an eye-witness account for the next radio bulletin. On the opposite side of the road from the explosion was the Scottish Office. I decided to go in and ask to borrow a phone from someone on reception. But when I got inside the hall there was no-one there. The entire front-of-house staff must have been outside on the pavement. So I just picked up the nearest phone, got through to Broadcasting House and recorded a piece from brief notes down the line for the news. A mini-scoop for me. When I came out, I met a colleague and together we started to walk back up the Embankment towards Parliament. We had not gone far when we heard another distant explosion. Turning round, we saw smoke rising from the Fleet Street area – we later found out it was a bomb which detonated outside the Old Bailey, injuring around 200 people. I recall we distanced ourselves immediately from the line of parked cars along the near side of the pavement and walked the rest of the way back on the river side. Any car could have contained a bomb. A few months later 8 members of the Belfast Brigade were given life sentences. There were 6 men and two women – the infamous Price sisters. The bombs marked the start of

Chapter Seven: To the Commons

a sustained campaign of IRA bombings on the British mainland – and led to a sharp tightening of security at Westminster.

Manure

There was another occasion, in 1978, when a couple, sitting in the public gallery, suddenly stood up, shouted some slogans, and threw some bags of horse manure into the chamber. The Scots Labour MP Tam Dalyell was on his feet at the time making a point of order* about the Scotland Bill, (as he often did) and when ordered to resume his seat by Speaker Thomas, looked down at the mess on the bench behind him and said, "I can't!" He said it was covered by "offensive material". Later some wag said George Thomas should have called "Ordure! Ordure!"

Working journalists at the House were not just reliant on MPs and peers as sources. Attendants, secretaries, personal assistants – all could be useful – and so could policemen. A group of them were stationed permanently in Parliament, based at Cannon Row. After the event I rushed to the office, wrote the story, and on my way to the BBC studio across the road - at the bottom of the Press Gallery lift - the

Chapter Seven: To the Commons

friendly copper on duty there, whom I knew well, said to me "You know who they are? – one of them is the daughter of the Prime Minister of Malta – Dom Mintoff". He knew this, he said, because he had been told it by a police colleague who had them in the cells. That was good enough for me, and when I got to the studio, I told the radio news editor down the line that I had a good source for saying who it was. But he wouldn't let me use it unless I had it confirmed by the Police Commander at Cannon Row. When I tried him, all I got was the usual "two people are helping police with their enquiries" – which we knew already. So that was another scoop that never happened. My police friend was right all along. Several days later Yana Mintoff and her colleague were charged with criminal damage to a carpet.

Airey Neave

This was a time when one lived with the lethal threat of attacks by the IRA on ministers and MPs at Westminster. The worst, for me, was the death **of** Airey Neave, the Conservative MP for Abingdon, decorated war hero, and close adviser of Mrs Thatcher. I had got to know him as chairman of the all-party committee on science and industry. When I once asked him if I could

Chapter Seven: To the Commons

make a film on the committee's work he agreed, and took me in his car one day to Harwell, near Abingdon, which is the centre of Britain's nuclear research. We made the film and drove back together. Then at the end of March 1979, two days after the Labour government of Jim Callaghan had lost a vote of confidence, and an election was in the offing, Airey was murdered within the Palace of Westminster. The INLA, a branch of the IRA, had placed a sophisticated explosive device under his car in the Commons underground car park. The device had a mercury tilt-mechanism detonator, so that as he drove up the ramp from a lower storey, his car was blown up. The sound could be heard in the Chamber. I recall the Conservative backbencher Peter Rees was in the middle of a speech during a Friday debate. Proceedings were adjourned and then resumed an hour later. Airey died at Westminster Hospital without regaining consciousness. Mrs Thatcher would certainly have made him Secretary of State for Northern Ireland when she came to power a month later – and there is no doubt Airey would have used much tougher methods in pursuing the IRA.

Chapter Seven: To the Commons

George Brown

In March 1976 I was a sad witness to the fall – in more ways than one - of George Brown. By then he was out of government and had been ennobled as Lord George-Brown. He summoned a press conference in his room in the House of Lords, to which Julian Haviland of ITN and I, together with some other lobby correspondents, went. George announced that he was resigning from the Labour Party (some years later he joined the SDP and became President of the Social Democratic Alliance). He said it was a protest against the government's plans to strengthen the closed shop. He was much the worse the wear for drink, which he could not handle. Someone remarked that he had only summoned up the courage to do this away from his formidable wife Sophie. Julian and I walked with him afterwards out of the Lords to go across to our studios on College Green for interviews. I seem to remember it had rained. As we stood on the kerb, Julian put a helping hand under George's elbow, which he roughly pushed away, and he then overbalanced, and fell sideways into the gutter. A camera flashed. It was a piteous sight. He was incoherent and could barely stand. I decided it would be impossible to interview him, and I believe Julian was of the same view. I went back to the office and told my editor. However, an early edition of a tabloid, I think the *Daily Mirror*, had arrived in ITN's newsroom before their bulletin with the damning photograph, and they made it into a big story. Where was the BBC's interview with George? There wasn't one. Big mistake by me. I should have done the interview, pathetic as it would have appeared, and then let the TV editors decide.

The Ron Browns

By an odd coincidence, I had an interesting encounter some years later. George had a brother called Ron, who was also a Labour MP, representing Hackney South and Shoreditch. His full name was Ronald William Brown.

When Roy Jenkins and 'the Gang of Four' broke away from Labour in early 1981 to form the Social Democratic Party, Ron Brown was one of a number of Labour MPs who defected to join them. His misfortune was that there was another Labour MP called Ron Brown – *his* full name was Ronald Duncan Brown – who sat for Edinburgh Leith. This latter Ron was an eccentric left-wing Scot who frequently got into trouble with the Speaker and had been suspended more than once. He was an electrician by trade.

Chapter Seven: To the Commons

Ron Brown, Hackney South and Shoreditch   *Ron Brown, Leith*

Shortly after the SDP was formed, I was in the Lobby and Ron from Leith called me over. "Hey, Peter, look at this", he said, and showed me an envelope addressed to Ron Brown MP at the House of Commons. Inside was a cheque made out to Ron Brown MP. I cannot now recall for how much. There was also a note which he showed me, something along the lines of "Dear Mr Brown, I think you are doing a great job and you have made the right decision and I hope the enclosed will help you". I regret I did not memorise the exact words. But what could I do? It was clearly delivered by the Commons officials to the wrong Ron Brown – they had put it in the wrong envelope sorting box in the Members' Lobby - but returning it was a matter

Chapter Seven: To the Commons

for him. It was not something I could report. I could not tell the other Ron Brown. I still do not know whether he passed the money back to the obvious recipient, who had joined a new party which Ron from Leith detested – or whether he even realised that it was not intended for himself.

A few years later, in 1988, the same Ron (from Leith) grabbed the mace and damaged it. He was suspended from the House for twenty days and had to pay for the repairs.

Albert Booth

In April 1976 I once did a story when luck and logic combined to give me a scoop. I was always the duty lobby man on Thursday mornings and went along for the BBC to the morning briefing at no.10 by the Prime Minister's press secretary. A reshuffle was in the offing. The Lobby were told that an announcement would be made later in the day, but it would only involve the Cabinet, not middle level ministers. I went back to the House and was walking down the committee corridor when I bumped into Albert Booth, then Minister of State* at the Department of Employment. His boss was Michael Foot. I knew Albert and liked him – a diligent MP who represented Barrow-in-Furness – and I had previously made a programme with him about his committee work (on Statutory Instruments). I said briefly to him "Are you in?" and he smiled and nodded, without saying very much. I deduced that this must mean that he was to be promoted to the Cabinet, and I guessed that Foot was moving on and that Albert, his deputy, would get Foot's job. With very little time to spare I rang the news editor and told him I was prepared to make a strong prediction for the one

Chapter Seven: To the Commons

o'clock news about the reshuffle. I did so, and I was right. Herograms all round!

The Circus

But politics is a game of swings and roundabouts. I got into deep trouble once when the Labour government was facing a vote of no confidence. On the Sunday before it occurred, I was rung by the Radio news editor and told to come in and do a piece about some Labour MPs who were threatening to abstain in the vote, according to the PA. Unfortunately I expressed some scepticism – the MPs were from what was known to some of us as "the Moncrieff circus" – MPs who would always give a quote to the redoubtable Political Editor of the Press Association, Chris Moncrieff, to make a Sunday story. I didn't want to go down that route and "stand it up", as the editor had requested. I argued that I was employed to exercise my judgement. The party whips* had yet to exert their pressure. But to no avail. It was on PA, it would be in the papers, so the BBC had to run the story too. Even if the MPs threatening to abstain changed their minds in the next few days. In retrospect, I should have rung up one or two of these MPs, gone in to Broadcasting House, and put some of my scepticism into the piece. Big mistake.

Churchill

One of the least pleasant aspects of being a political correspondent was being woken up in the night or (in an era before mobile phones) rung on a 'pager'* and told to get dressed and get into work. This usually happened when I was duty weekend correspondent, after the Sunday papers

Chapter Seven: To the Commons

had arrived in Broadcasting House between 12 and 1 on a Sunday morning. On one occasion in 1979 the solicitors of Winston Churchill, the MP grandson of the great Sir Winston Churchill, issued a statement admitting that he had had an affair with a lady called Soraya Khashoggi, wife of the wealthy international arms dealer. Apparently, this had been mentioned in a trial of three Scotland Yard detectives. The affair had been going on for some time, and Churchill was married to Minnie D'Erlanger, daughter of a former chairman of BOAC. But why was the news released at this unearthly hour? I reckon it was aimed to come after the last deadline in Fleet Street, thus avoiding front page headlines. But for the early morning radio news bulletins, it was perfect. But there was one big disadvantage - there was no-one available at that time – neither Winston nor Soraya nor solicitors - ready or willing to answer the phone. I broke the news, but it wasn't the sort of story I enjoyed doing. But when Mrs Thatcher won the next election, there was no job for Winston.

Chapter Seven: To the Commons

Fig. 32 BBC Parliamentary Team, present and former members 1988 ((back row from left) Peter Hill. Christopher Jones, Brian Curtois (front row) Rodney Foster, David Holmes, Peter Hardiman Scott, Conrad Voss Bark

Chapter Eight: Thatcher in No.10

Blunt

When Mrs Thatcher came to power one of the first things she did, on 20th November 1979, was to unveil the fact that the former Surveyor of the Queen's Pictures had been a Russian spy. Sir Anthony Blunt had been interrogated by MI5 a number of times, but had been given immunity, and had not been put on trial. A book had appeared the previous year, written by a BBC producer, Andrew Boyle, which hinted at Blunt's past without actually naming him. The Prime Minister's statement was a sensation. Blunt gave a long interview to BBC TV News, and I did a Parliamentary report on the exchanges in the Commons, which followed the interview in the Six O'Clock News. That whole bulletin is

Chapter Eight: Thatcher in No. 10

preserved in the BBC TV Archives, thus giving me a digital immortality. A Labour MP, Ted Leadbitter, had agreed to put a planted question, and the Prime Minister had a frank and factual reply ready. Apparently, Mrs Thatcher said to Leadbitter afterwards, "And it damn well serves him right".

Sir Tom Williams

Perhaps I should mention a story I felt ambivalent about, that happened one evening in the summer of 1981, shortly after the SDP had broken away from the Labour Party. They were looking for seats to fight. My friend David Mellor, who was a barrister and a Tory MP, told me almost as an aside that a Labour MP, Sir Tom Williams QC (a distinguished Labour lawyer) was going to be made a judge. I did not react, but immediately realised there would have to be a by-election in a Labour seat. There was not much time before the evening news bulletin. I managed to get Tom Williams on the phone. He was very shocked that I knew. "Who told you? How did this get out? Quintin [the Lord Chancellor, Lord Hailsham] doesn't like leaks. Please don't broadcast this now – wait till it is official". I was in a quandary. I discussed it with a colleague, Noel Lewis. Apparently Sir Tom had not been well, and very much wanted to go to the judge's bench. I had no doubt the story was true, but should I run with it? From the human point of view, it might ruin Sir Tom Williams' chances if the Lord Chancellor did change his mind. Noel suggested ways of writing it which would tone it down, but in the end, I decided one man's future was worth more than another man's short-lived scoop. I have discussed this dilemma at journalists' training

Chapter Eight: Thatcher in No. 10

schools, and the majority view has always been that I should have reported it. And I think I probably should. I was never hard-nosed enough. Anyway, when it was officially announced, Roy Jenkins ran for the SDP at Warrington that July, amid massive press coverage, and lost by fewer than 2000 votes to Doug Hoyle (father of the current Speaker). Sir Tom was made a circuit judge and died five years later.

The Falklands War

One of the few times that the Commons has ever met on a Saturday was immediately after the Argentinians invaded the Falklands in 1982. The BBC was broadcasting Parliamentary debates by then, and Radio 4 was cleared for the day. It was Saturday 3rd April. It was my role to provide the commentary from the small glass-fronted box at the end of the Commons chamber – the Commentary Box*. Some colleagues used to complain about the fleas supposedly brought in by police sniffer dogs which checked the small booth for explosives before the Commons sat. We were expecting a two-hour debate, which I had prepared to introduce, but the first thing that happened in the chamber was that someone moved a motion that this time should be considerably extended. A vote was called, and the House immediately divided. I suddenly found I had fifteen minutes of unexpected silence to fill. "Keep talking", my producer Peter Robbins said in my ear, and as I stumbled on from my prepared notes, he would chime in with "You're doing fine" or "We can go to music if you dry up!" I managed about twelve minutes. The debate itself was immensely dramatic, but one of the most tense exchanges was when a Tory

Chapter Eight: Thatcher in No. 10

backbencher, Ray Whitney, who had previously served as a diplomat in the British Embassy in Buenos Aires, was arguing in favour of diplomatic negotiations with Argentina. He was accused of defeatism by a right-wing colleague, Sir John Biggs-Davison. He also shouted "This is treason!" at him. I heard it on my earphones, though Hansard did not, or chose not to report his actual words. But it occurred, alas, during the only five minutes of the whole live broadcast when we cut away for the one o'clock news. At least I was able to describe it later. The art of these live broadcasts was fitting any commentary in between the pauses in the MPs' speeches. As an aside – something which shows the then continuing power of radio – a naval colleague told me that during the debate, officers at the Royal Naval College in Dartmouth were so keen to follow the debate they sat in a circle around a radio set in the wardroom.

Trenchard

During the Falklands war I reported in May on the radio news and on "*Today*" that HMS *Sheffield*, which had been hit by an Exocet missile, had originally been designed with greater length to incorporate anti-air missiles, but then its size, and therefore its armament, was cut back for reasons of economy. I had this from a document provided by the government to the Commons Defence Committee. So it was already in the public domain*. And it was the subject of a question in the House of Lords by Lord Mayhew a day later. I had been a naval officer during National Service, so I was familiar with what I was talking about. But Lord Trenchard, the Minister for Defence Procurement, was

84

Chapter Eight: Thatcher in No. 10

furious. In reply to a letter from me he said he had called for a transcript and named myself and Peter Donaldson (whose only crime was reading the news that morning), and suggested we were undermining the morale of the relatives of those killed during the attack (more than 20 sailors were killed). He also wrote a long letter to the BBC Chairman, George Howard, which began "Dear George", but Howard roundly rejected his criticism and expressed complete confidence in the information. He added that a poll had found that 81% of the public approved of the BBC's coverage. I was told by a senior member of the Commons Defence Committee that they would be meeting the following morning behind closed doors to discuss the ship and its armament. He obviously forgot this conversation, as he later asked me how I had found out about the committee session. I could have said "From you", but I didn't. The Commons Defence Committee thought one of its members had leaked the story to me. Unfortunately, I heard next day that when they met, one of their number, a Tory MP called Sir Patrick Wall, had to leave the meeting early, just before one. They thought it was him. But it wasn't. The funny thing was that he was going off to a studio to do an interview for *The World at One* about the story. I am glad to say Alan Protheroe, then Deputy D-G, stood behind me throughout. Shortly afterwards the MP who had pointed me towards the Defence Committee report walked past me in a corridor, and said out of the side of his mouth, without breaking step, "Don't talk to me for a month!" And in later years whenever I and my good newsreader friend met, we would exclaim "Donaldson and Hill!"

Chapter Eight: Thatcher in No. 10

The Honours List

A few months later, in October, a special Falklands Honours List came out. The normal procedure was for a representative of each news organisation to go to Downing Street, where there was a special briefing on the names to look for and highlight, after which we signed a solemn declaration that we would not broadcast or print them until after a fixed time. This gave a period during which newsrooms could research and write their stories. I personally was there to sign on behalf of the BBC for four copies - for the D-G, the World Service, the TV newsroom and the radio newsroom. The lists contained the award of two V.C.s for action in the Falklands, to Colonel 'H' Jones, who commanded 2PARA, and who died at Goose Green, and to Sergeant Ian Mackay. Unfortunately, the 'Sun' decided to break the undertaking, and to splash the news of the V.C.s on their next front page. What to do? I argued that I had given my word that the BBC would keep the list secret until the appropriate time. But David Holmes, the then Political Editor, gave wiser counsel. "They are now in the public domain," he said, "through no action of ours, and therefore we should go ahead and report it."

Chapter Eight: Thatcher in No. 10

And so we did. The 'Sun' was banned from the Lobby for several months.

I still have a copy of 'Lobby Practice', a small book which lays out clear rules of behaviour. Rule 5 states: "The Lobby regularly receives Advance Copies of official documents to facilitate its work. All embargoes on such documents, and on all information given orally or operationally in advance for the Lobby's convenience, must be strictly observed." It looks as though the editor of the Sun overruled his Political Correspondent.

The Lobby

The rules also state that one should never identify an informant without permission or reveal anything which could lead to their identification. One should not talk about lobby meetings, "see" anything in the Members' Lobby, run after a Minister, or write about something accidentally overheard. These rules have often been criticised, for the cult of secrecy, by those who want a more open political society and all official statements on the record; but as the case of the Falkland War honours shows, the rules have a value in ensuring fairness between all media outlets and the observance of common deadlines. When they are breached, trust between governments and MPs on the one hand, and political reporters on the other, is fractured. And the public – readers, listeners and viewers – learn less.

Chapter Eight: Thatcher in No. 10

Ronald Reagan

In June 1982 when President Ronald Reagan visited Britain and addressed both houses in the Royal Gallery, I did the live commentary with John Hosken. What the President had to say was unremarkable – part of it was about the threat of international communism - but *how* he did it fascinated both peers and MPs. He spoke from two slanting pieces of glass on stands, which reflected a rolling autocue from two monitors on the floor. This was the first time, to my knowledge, that the system had ever been used by a politician in Britain. When the great and good had departed, a large part of the audience of MPs and peers, instead of leaving, surged forward, to see how he did it so naturally. Nowadays, it is commonplace for all political leaders to use it at party conferences and elsewhere on public platforms.

Chapter Eight: Thatcher in No. 10

Brighton Bomb

A great regret was that in October 1984 I, and several other BBC correspondents, slept through the Brighton bomb. Unfortunately, we had been accommodated in a hotel quite a long way along the Prom from the Grand Hotel – and we heard nothing. It was only when we turned on our morning radios that we discovered what had happened half a mile away. My good friend and colleague John Harrison happened to be relaxing in the Metropole Hotel next door to the Grand with his film crew, after doing a piece for the next morning's TV news – and so was on hand to put together a terrific exclusive report – shots of the collapsed hotel front, and half the Cabinet on the promenade in their dressing gowns - that won several media prizes. ITV had sent their crew back to London. I recall John Cole getting a spirited interview with Mrs Thatcher in the local police station, and her fighting talk from the platform as the conference re-assembled. Five people were killed in the bombing and over thirty injured, some seriously. The bomber, Patrick Magee, was eventually

Chapter Eight: Thatcher in No. 10

caught and given eight concurrent life sentences, though, to the anger of many, he was released under licence in 1999.

Whitelaw

On another occasion in the early 80s I got one of those 1 a.m. phone calls at home. "Peter, there's a story in today's *Telegraph* about Willie Whitelaw...." I can't remember the details other than that it was about immigration. Willie, then Home Secretary, had addressed the Tory backbench Home Affairs Committee and told them something new. I was actually outside the room in the Committee corridor when the meeting broke up, but Whitelaw's press spokesman – Derek Howe – had nothing to tell me, or any of the other journalists waiting there. It was a private meeting, he insisted. I didn't suspect anything. Perhaps I should have done. Because Willie had obviously briefed – or authorised a briefing – to the *Telegraph's* man. And to him only. I had a difficult decision – do I just report what had appeared in the paper, at second hand, or could I "stand it up", as no doubt I was asked to

Chapter Eight: Thatcher in No. 10

do. In the end I plucked up courage and rang Whitelaw's home. Waking up a Home Secretary was not something I had much experience of. Mrs Whitelaw picked up the phone and told me briskly that he was asleep, and she was not going to disturb him. End of story. Disaster – for me. But that's how exclusives happen – ministers now and then leak to their favourite newspaper or lobby man. They know the audience they want for their story. And there's not much you can do about it.

Kinnock

Around 1988/89 I ran into trouble when Neil Kinnock was trying to turn the Labour party against unilateral nuclear disarmament, after it had lost three consecutive General Elections. He made a speech on a Sunday, saying Labour wasn't entirely opposed to nuclear weapons and favoured international talks on multilateral disarmament. It had not been "flashed up" by his press office in advance as important, as often happens with major speeches. I rang the Labour party press spokesman about it, and he drew my

Chapter Eight: Thatcher in No. 10

attention to a speech Neil had made previously, setting out roughly the same position. So it clearly wasn't new. Or so I believed. I rang the newsroom and told them so. But then on the early evening ITN News, their Political Correspondent, Michael Brunson, who carried a lot of weight, led their bulletin and said, in effect, this was a major turning point for Labour. That made me look very foolish. He may not have been right, but on a thin news day, the fact that Brunson said it was news, *made* it news. And he carried a lot more clout than me. I went in to Broadcasting House and did a piece about it, but we had lost the advantage. Sometimes there's no virtue in being right; best to swallow your pride and do what you're told. At a meeting of the party's NEC in May 1989 Kinnock persuaded the executive to make the shift away from unilateralism part of their permanent policy. He still lost the next election.

Chapter Nine: Problems with Benn

Chesterfield

I did have what I thought was a real scoop - on Tony Benn in 1984 – only to find it turn to dust. I had yet another of those middle-of-the-night phone calls. The radio newsroom. They told me they had received information that Tony Benn, who had previously lost his Parliamentary seat at Bristol, and was looking to be selected for the safe Labour seat of Chesterfield (where Eric Varley had resigned), had failed to get onto the shortlist. Sensation! But how could I, at around 2am in Twickenham, confirm it? A few minutes later I got a call from the Labour MP Chris Mullin, Editor of *Tribune* and a close associate of Benn.

Chapter Nine: Problems with Benn

He had rung the newsroom who had given him my number. He told me it was true. To prove it, I ask him to name the six who had been selected for the shortlist, which he did. It was rather surprising how he knew. As it happens one of them was Phillip Whitehead, the former Labour MP for Derby North, and a good friend of mine. So I rang Phillip in the early morning and asked him if was true. "Yes," he replied, "but we were all sworn to secrecy till the Chesterfield Labour Party announce the shortlist on Monday." Benn, honouring the letter but not the spirit of the promise, had probably got Mullin to leak it for him. The aim was clearly to cause a hullabaloo and get the decision reversed. According to a good source, Benn had already tried to block Phillip (who was Kinnock's preferred candidate) by getting a member of the selection committee to ask all the candidates if they had ever been a member of another party – knowing full well that Phillip had been a Tory at Oxford. Around 7am I got hold of the Chesterfield party chairman on the phone, and he was deeply shocked that I knew. But the core facts were right. I rang the radio newsroom and told them I had a scoop. But would you believe it, the editor would not run it till it was confirmed by another news source. Later in the morning another reporter was sent round to Benn's house in Holland Park, Benn confirmed it, and it was run at 1pm. Was I annoyed! And Benn achieved his purpose, because it created a fuss, he was put back on the list, and eventually he became the MP for the seat. This is not, of course, how it is recounted in Benn's memoirs, though it is true. Triumph for him, disaster for me.

Chapter Nine: Problems with Benn

Deputy Leadership

A further middle-of-the-night adventure, also involving Benn, had happened to me three years earlier, in 1981. I was the duty all-night man at the Commons. I was left covering a long committee session to do with telephones. All the gallery men had gone home. Around 1 or 2 am the Press Gallery attendant put his head round the door of the BBC office. "Tony Benn's just been up with a statement", he said. I rushed out. It announced that Benn intended to run against Denis Healey for the Deputy Leadership of the Labour Party.

Odd timing, but big news. I went down immediately to the Lobby where I found Phillip Whitehead, Austin Mitchell, Jack Straw and Robin Cook. When I showed them the statement, they were furious. Apparently, Benn had joined the Tribune Group*, of which they were well-known members, and had promised he would not run without consulting them first. I asked them who would be a good

Chapter Nine: Problems with Benn

spokesman to oppose the move, and they suggested John Silkin. I got a reporter down to the Commons from the *Today* programme to do an interview, and they got a strong reaction from him. I rang Benn's office in the Commons once or twice, but all I could get from him was "I shtand by my shtatement". Fortunately, there was a division around 6am (those were the crazy hours the Commons used to keep), and after the vote I confronted Benn personally in a corridor. He still refused. I then told him the BBC had already secured an interview with Silkin. His whole demeanour changed. "But he could be a candidate!" he exploded (and he was right – Silkin did stand); however, he agreed to give an interview to the *Today* reporter. Come the morning bulletins I had a wonderful scoop, there was nothing in the morning papers, and the *Today* programme wrapped up all the details of what developed into a major split in the party; at the subsequent party conference, in the autumn of 1981, Healey defeated Benn by less than one percent (50.4% to Benn's 49.6%). Needless to say, once again, my account here is somewhat at variance with the version that appears in Mr Benn's memoirs. But mine is true. For once, a small triumph.

Obituary

In 1992 I left the BBC staff and went freelance. I gained a number of contracts – with the Foreign Office (looking after visiting dignitaries), and with EMI* (compiling a CD of 'Great Parliamentary Speeches'). The latter took some time, but was much encouraged by the then Speaker, Jack Weatherill, who recommended to me some speeches he had

Chapter Nine: Problems with Benn

heard from the chair, when few MPs, or reporters, were present. Among those I included was a speech by Tony Benn. When the CD, which I recorded at EMI's Abbey Road studios, finally came out, the BBC held a party at the Commons, and Mr Speaker Weatherill helped launch it with a little speech of his own.

Now it happened that day that I had been at TV Centre rewriting Tony Benn's obituary. It was referred to me after an interesting exchange. Someone in Radio News had already written a rather hostile, unfair obit of Benn, from a distinctly right-wing point of view. It was lying in the files. Someone else, presumably also in Radio News, had come across it and then leaked it to Tony Benn. I do not know who, but I came across such insider leaking elsewhere in the BBC, mostly to aid the far left of politics. On receiving it, Benn had then written a number of corrections in the margin of the original document and sent it back, to the Director-General. The D-G then sent it to the Editor of Radio News, with a note attached 'I am sure you will know exactly what to do with it!'. It was finally given to me, and I wrote a much fairer, and I hope, more balanced view of Benn's journey from Westminster School and an inherited peerage to Labour minister and hard-left campaigner.

So after doing my revision I went to the party. I got a drink, and then who should I find myself in conversation with but – Tony Benn. He did not ask me what I had been up to that day. And I was not striving to tell him. I wonder what would have happened if I had!

Chapter Nine: Problems with Benn

I was for many years aware of the importance of having ready-made obituaries, from the day in 1963 when President John F. Kennedy was assassinated in Dallas. I was working in the Overseas Service at Bush House. We had nothing prepared. Indeed, we had no obituaries written on any world leader. A very able producer, Raymond Barker, sat down immediately and wrote one from his own knowledge in record time. He later became a Lecturer in Politics at Bradford.

And some time later I remember, in November 1974, the newsroom rang our office at the Commons and said John Stonehouse, a Labour minister, was presumed dead, after his clothes had been found on a beach. Of course, we later discovered he had faked his own death and disappeared. But at the time the newsroom wanted an immediate profile-cum-obituary. We had no system then, and nothing prepared. Between us, we scrambled something together for the lunchtime bulletin! Stonehouse turned up some years later in Australia with his mistress.

Chapter Nine: Problems with Benn

After I had begun systematically to write obituaries of our most important politicians, there were one or two occasions when my efforts *were* justified. One was in 1993 when I woke up around seven o'clock in the morning and turned the radio on – to hear my own voice. I was talking about the life, and death, of the former Liberal leader Jo Grimond. It was something of a shock, but the system had worked – my prepared tape had been played, without my involvement.

And when John Smith, the Scottish Labour MP who briefly led the Labour party, died of a heart attack in May 1994, and it was announced in mid-morning, my ready-for-use obituary was put out. As was a rather longer obituary of Harold Wilson, when he died in 1995. It was included in the *'Today'* programme, giving the producers time to get leading politicians to the phone. I continued preparing obituaries well into the 1990s, so that radio news built up a good stock, and because of the different demands of news, particularly when Radio 5 began, I edited important ones down to fit

Chapter Nine: Problems with Benn

shorter bulletins. Important politicians, like, say, Roy Jenkins, would have three different versions ready, for use on Radio 2, Radio 4, or Radio 5 Live. Their news bulletins were all of different lengths. Also with new technology, the formats on which I recorded changed, from discs to tape to cassettes to miniaturised MP3s*, meaning I often had to re-record and revise obits already done. Of course, the smaller the format, the more it reduced storage problems in the BBC's large Archives. I admit I sometimes prepared obituaries of politicians who were not in the front rank, but whom I had always admired, or had got on well with. Arthur Bottomley was one; Eric Heffer was another. Eric had stomach cancer and finally attended the Commons in a wheelchair. At his last appearance, John Major crossed the floor to shake his hand. In May 1991 I went to a cricket match at Lords. It was a Bank Holiday, so from a news point of view, not much was going on. When I got home, I said to my wife, "Anything happened?" and she said, "You were second item on the 6 O' Clock News!" Why? because Eric had died, and in the absence of other news, he was near the top of the running order. On a busy day, he would have been much further down. So, I was glad: I did my bit for him!

Eventually I had to stop doing obits, as I was getting far older than current leading politicians. I was reminded of this once, when I was sitting in the BBC Office in the Press Gallery, a couple of yards away from the desk of the Political Editor, John Cole. He was on the phone. "No! No! No!" he was saying to someone in his rich Ulster accent. When he finished, I asked him what that was all about. "They want me to write an obit for TV of Chris Patten" (who had been

Chapter Nine: Problems with Benn

a Northern Ireland minister and had held several Ministerial posts for the Conservatives). He went on: "I'm much older than he is and likely to die much earlier, so if I do an obit and they eventually put it out, people will ask about me, 'Where's he broadcasting from?'".

As it happens, I was in the BBC office once towards 6pm when John suddenly fell backwards. He had had a heart attack. The Editor of 'Hansard' swiftly arrived, and performed first aid, in which he was trained; then the House of Commons nurse, who ordered a wheelchair to get him down to the ground floor in the lift. As they went out, John asked me to go with him. I accompanied him in the ambulance, and later in the acute ward, where he was attached to several machines. I stayed by him until his family arrived. A short time later John had a heart bypass operation, and within months was back at work. Some years later as we went out into the Press Gallery together John clapped me on the shoulder: "Do you know what day it is today?" he asked me. "No," I replied. "It's exactly five years to the day since I had my heart attack!" he answered, with a big smile.

Chapter Ten: Ups and Downs as a Freelance

YIP

After I left the BBC staff I continued as a freelance to present *Yesterday in Parliament (YIP)* on Radio 4 for several years in the 1990s. I enjoyed this, even though it meant not getting home until around 1am. We had to wait until the live transmission of *Today in Parliament (TIP)* was over. My brief was to try and make the presentation more lively and less formal than it had traditionally been, rather than a simple repeat of the programme of the night before. When I started, the script was read out by a newsreader sent down to Westminster from the Presentation Department. I often included extracts from the House of Lords, where some of the more eccentric speeches were made. My most daring diversion from reality was when P.D.James, the famous author of murder stories (and a Governor of the BBC), was ennobled. At the end of the programme I said something like this: "And as Baroness James left the Chamber, the Lord Speaker slumped slowly forward on the Woolsack*, and in his back could be seen – a silver stiletto! No, I'm only joking". To my surprise the editor of the programme, Matt Morris, thought it was funny and left it in. When the programme reached its end next morning on Radio 4, John Humphrys said "I assure you; he *was* joking!"

Chapter Ten: Ups and Downs as a Freelance

Two Scots Part

Another freelance contract I had after leaving the staff was to work for the new digital *BBC News Online*. My brief was to write robust profiles of MPs and MSPs for the website. Over two years I wrote around 700 of them. Because of devolution, there were far more than just the Westminster MPs. A new acronym soup had been cooked up. There were English MPs, Welsh MS, Stormont MLAs, and Scots MSPs. Not to mention the MEPs in Strasbourg. There was little interest, and barely any editorial control, over what I was writing: the management was happy for me just to get on with it. All of it was put up online in the Politics section of the website. On one occasion I was researching some MSPs, and I found online a report in a Scottish newspaper, with a headline which said that two MSPs, who were married to each other, were going to separate. I put this into their profiles. But I did not read the story far enough down, to realise that it was a spoof headline, ironic rather than factual, and that what was really happening was that the two MSPs were going to be apart for a few weeks while they fought an election in constituencies in different parts of Scotland. They were distanced from each other. But their marriage remained intact.

Their reaction when it appeared on the BBC website was strong, and everyone in Edinburgh from the Controller BBC Scotland downwards was annoyed to discover that an Englishman in London was writing (albeit on a national U.K.-wide website) about their own Scottish representatives (and in this particular case, getting it wrong). They may have

Chapter Ten: Ups and Downs as a Freelance

feared a libel writ. I offered to write personally to the two MSPs and apologise and explain how it happened; but this was rejected: it was all taken out of my hands. It was a genuine mistake. Later all my profiles were removed from the website. Some were a little too robust for the MPs I wrote about. One Conservative MP objected to me writing that he had been fined for environmental offences, that he had asked questions in the House about a subject for which he had been paid by a PR firm, and that he lived in a large mansion. All were true, and I felt this was the sort of information his constituents should know. But he felt this was not the sort of thing the BBC should be doing. He objected to my profile of him, stood up in the 1922 Committee, and asked other Tory MPs to read what I had written about them and to complain about me to the Director-General. I was told this by an MP who was there.

LOVE and HATE

Another MP, a former trade unionist, was reported in a book by a scrupulous colleague, Andrew Roth, to have had the letters L.O.V.E. and H.A.T.E. tattooed on his knuckles, and when he became an MP, to have had them surgically removed. I rang the MP's office to try to get it confirmed or denied; they said they would ring back. They did not. I rang again, and again, and still could not get a straight answer. I finally wrote that this event had been reported elsewhere, a little short of saying it was true. Although I suspect, from the MP's failure to use the several opportunities I gave him to deny it, that it was. I believed that it was my job to let constituents know about what their MPs were really like:

Chapter Ten: Ups and Downs as a Freelance

how often they spoke, what their outside business interests were, what free trips they went on, and so on, as well as their contributions to debate and votes against the party line. MPs, in my view, were very self-regarding, and self-protective, especially when it came to their outside interests and free tickets. But BBC managers did not want to upset the apple cart. The small fuss over my profiles was as nothing to the explosion of public anger when in May 2009 the *Daily Telegraph* published the expenses files of Members and peers, and their many attempts to misuse the public purse. Some of them finished up in gaol, several resigned, several decided not to stand again, and many repaid money falsely claimed.

Complaints were made about me and my profiles; and with the approach of the BBC Charter Renewal*, the men in suits took the easy option. They did not want to imperil their future finance, which depended on the approval of ministers and MPs. But I had been given a clear brief when I was hired: the profiles were to be truthful, and not a watered-down version of *Who's Who,* where the entries were supplied by the subjects. I took the view (as did those who commissioned me at *News on Line*) that in a democracy voters are entitled to know the facts about their MPs, and their backgrounds. But there were those, even in the BBC, who disagreed. When I wrote profiles of British MEPs in Strasbourg, in which I included all their outside business interests, paid-for trips and so on, I sent them to the BBC man in Strasbourg to check. He was mildly shocked, and his reply was that I should not be doing this (even though I had done it for Westminster MPs).

Chapter Ten: Ups and Downs as a Freelance

The Liberal MEPs had already published a voluntary register of outside earnings and business interests, and it was not very hard to persuade the Labour MEPs to follow suit. The Conservative MEPs were more resistant, and they debated it internally, but eventually their press officer, without comment, sent me a full list of their business interests. This was a good step forward in openness, as it was not an enforceable requirement; and I had played a part in making it happen. Previously the lists were kept in a book which could be inspected in an office to which few were admitted, even if they knew where it was. Regrettably, the view of my Strasbourg colleague was also that of senior BBC people back in London, and the profiles of our Members of the European Parliament were also pulled. It was a brief too far.

So, with BBC charter renewal approaching, and with the management under political pressure from the MPs who could determine these matters, the head of *News on Line* was ordered from on high to remove every single profile I had written. There were 650 of them, plus around 200 for the three devolved parliaments and Europe, and it had taken me 2 years at least to write them. The manager who had hired me and given me a brief to write incisively, was as displeased as I was to have this very useful part of his website closed down.

Chapter Ten: Ups and Downs as a Freelance

CD and Dods

Fortunately, before I left, a friendly engineer, and an expert in IT, seeing me looking glum, stopped by my desk in the TV Centre, and asked if he could help in any way. I said it would be nice to have a record of all my work in the previous two years. He said, "I will see what I can do". A week or two later a padded envelope arrived through my letterbox. Inside was a CD, and on it was every single political profile I had written. There was no covering letter. When I later went to work for Dods, a publishing house which produced heavyweight political annuals, in the run up to a coming General Election, the CD proved extremely useful. There was a demand for online personal information about the backgrounds of not just MPs standing again, but of candidates of the other political parties, some of whom might become new MPs. In truth, I had barely touched on what was really going on. Nobody at the time knew about the manipulation of expenses through the Commons Fees Office*. But, as in many things, *BBC News on Line* was ahead of its time.

Political CDs

But now and then good fortune came my way. An executive from EMI was driving in to work, and he heard on his car radio a programme I had broadcast one morning on the highlights of my time in the Gallery, some of the best and most interesting speeches I had heard since the BBC started recording Parliament in 1978. It had the title, I think, of 'Echoes from the Chamber'. He asked to see me and wondered whether I could put together a CD at greater

Chapter Ten: Ups and Downs as a Freelance

length – perhaps two hours – of outstanding speeches in the Commons and the Lords between April 1978 and May 1994.

The BBC, BBC Archives, Hansard and EMI came to an agreement, and I started work. It was fascinating. Often the Hansard written version varied quite a bit from the actual transmission. Words that I had heard from the Gallery, often off-mike, were never officially written down. A remark like "silly bugger!" or "absolute balls!" would be ignored by the Speaker, although I had clearly heard it from the Gallery, and it never made it into Hansard. The only exceptions were when someone across the Chamber reacted to the remark. The broadcasting of Parliament could sometimes embarrass MPs. On one occasion a Tory MP denied in the House that he had said something, and the Labour MP Willie Hamilton rose and said "Mr Speaker, I have just been across to the BBC offices and listened to the tape, and the Honourable Member's expression is clearly audible!".

Great Parliamentary Speeches

Some of the speeches on my CD, like the Falklands debate, and Mrs Thatcher's farewell, I had heard myself; others were suggested by MPs, including the then Speaker, Jack Weatherill, who became an enthusiast for the project and put forward a number of ideas. I wrote to several ministers and asked them what speeches had impressed them. After a lot of editing and cutting, I settled on two and a half hours of speeches – 105 different recordings – some witty, some sad, some moving, some very excited. I had followed the John West canned fish principle – the quality was assured by the bits you throw away! The title was '*Great Parliamentary*

Chapter Ten: Ups and Downs as a Freelance

Speeches'. We had a good party to launch the CD and it led to other things. I did a big round of interviews, many with local radio stations about the MPs from their region whom I had included – not always to their advantage.

Great Political Speeches

Two years later some more good fortune came my way. I was approached by an editor from Hodder, the publishers,* who had a large Spoken Word section, where actors or authors read their books onto tape or CDs.

This time, the idea was for me to dig into the BBC Archives and find political speeches from the past and link them together. They ranged from an early recording of Gladstone

Chapter Ten: Ups and Downs as a Freelance

on a wax cylinder, through Asquith, Lloyd George and McDonald, to Chamberlain, Churchill, and Bevin and ending in the era of Blair*, Howard and Heseltine. Nearly all of them were speeches made outside the Commons: at party conferences, in overseas assemblies, miners' galas or election meetings. The only speaker with whom I had trouble was Sir Winston Churchill: negotiating copyright payments with his literary agents was not easy. He had re-recorded some of his Commons speeches for Decca, and to use these, or extracts from them, needed the consent of his literary executors. And they wanted considerable payments.

GREAT POLITICAL SPEECHES
Selected from over 100 years of archive recordings
PRODUCED IN ASSOCIATION WITH BBC NEWS

Chapter Ten: Ups and Downs as a Freelance

The recorded speeches lack the spontaneous reactions of MPs in the chamber, or voices from an audience; but they are unmistakeable, rhetorical and profound. Some of the later speeches on my CDs include phrases that have become familiar: "Back to Basics"; "On yer Bike"; and "The Lady's NOT for turning!".

This second CD, issued by Hodder Headline, was called *'Great Political Speeches'* and won the Best Non-Fiction award for spoken word in *The Talkies* for 1997. There was a ceremony in a big London hotel, and I did another round of radio interviews to promote it. The extract the promoters chose to introduce my CD at the ceremony was a hellfire speech in a Belfast chapel by Rev. Ian Paisley; I got a laugh in my acceptance speech by asking the audience, if they ever met him, not to tell him about this choice!

Sound Recording

Sound recording began with Edison's phonograph - wax cylinders, intended for use by business executives. Nowadays the formats have changed. When I started in the

Chapter Ten: Ups and Downs as a Freelance

BBC, at Bush House, we cut vinyl discs as we spoke to the microphone live in the studio; then came ¼ inch tape machines, then cassettes, then digital MP3, and CDs. My latest laptop does not have a CD facility. Everything has gone digital. At least in that respect, John Birt as BBC Director-General was ahead of his time. I once researched the history of sound recording for an article in *'British Journalism Review'* and it was interesting that before the war nearly all programmes were live. A Recorded Programmes Executive was appointed. In the late Twenties an internal memo asked why they could not try to 'bottle programmes and uncork them later'. With the expansion of overseas programmes and the Empire Service, it was necessary to put the same programme out to parts of the world in different time zones; hence the need to cut shellac discs which could be transmitted at different times of day. I believe Neville Chamberlain's announcement that Britain was at war with Germany was recorded on a machine in Maida Vale known as a Blattnerphone, which could record half an hour of material on a steel tape which weighed over twenty pounds. During the war many BBC correspondents with the armies in Europe travelled in a van with an engineer and cut discs describing what they had seen. It was not until a German recording machine, called the Magnetophon, was captured in Norway towards the end of the war, that the value of recording on tape was realised by BBC producers. It took several years for BBC Administration to accept that this represented an improvement in quality of sound and ease of use. But eventually they became the standard for decades.

Chapter Ten: Ups and Downs as a Freelance

Finding Orwell's Voice

Researching the records in BBC Archives took me down an unusual path. Because of a personal link with his family, I had always been interested in George Orwell, and as a freelance I wrote several articles about his private diaries, which are held in a library in London University. Orwell had been a producer in the BBC in the early part of the war, in the Eastern Service, broadcasting to India. He produced plays and talks by well-known people. But he also read weekly current affairs commentaries himself, and chaired discussions of literature and poetry. So what did his voice sound like? He had been shot in the throat during the Spanish Civil War, and he suffered from progressive lung disease, as he smoked his own roll-ups. Contemporaries said his voice was high and not good for broadcasting. But there were no Orwell recordings in Archives. I appealed for help, particularly to engineers,

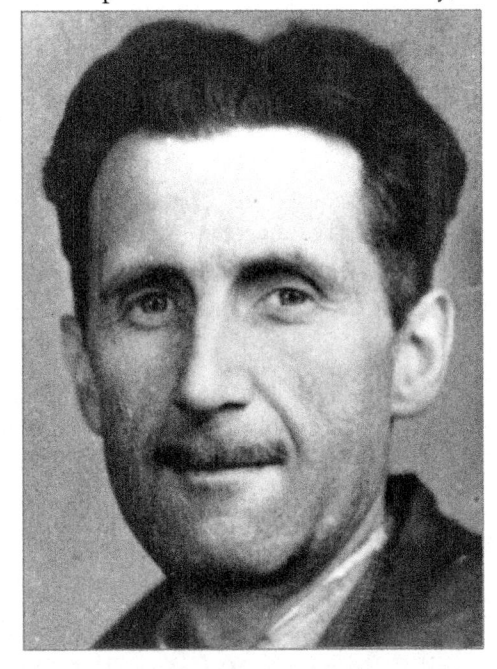

Chapter Ten: Ups and Downs as a Freelance

through the BBC's own magazine for its pensioners, *Prospero*.

I tried hard to find a recording of him, as none were known to exist. I went through the catalogue of the US Library of Congress, with the aid of the Reference Librarian, on the names of both Orwell and Blair without success. I contacted radio authorities in India and Germany, in case they had recorded his broadcasts during the war, and I went carefully through the BBC's own sound archives. The editor of Orwell's collected works, Prof. Peter Davison, gave me some recording numbers for Orwell's discs, but I could not find them. I was contacted by a former BBC engineer, Douglas Moyle, who had fought with Orwell in Spain. Douglas is mentioned several times in 'Homage to Catalonia'. He told me Orwell's voice at the microphone was 'weak and shaky'.

The lack of a surviving recording is best explained by David Martin, a former Recorded Programmes assistant at the BBC from 1942 onwards. He told me that he had handled thousands of the 12" metal discs, coated with cellulose acetate, which were played on a gramophone with a steel needle. He said that the metal was a scarce and valuable resource at this time, and most of the discs were recycled or melted down after use. I was referred to a German collector, Bernard Wichert, who had a huge private archive of recordings; he said to me that he had done a similar search and drawn a blank.

My final hope came from a letter which Orwell wrote to a BBC Features producer, Rayner Heppenstall, in 1947, about

Chapter Ten: Ups and Downs as a Freelance

a radio play he had produced. In it he said: "I expected the discs would be scrapped, however. I had them illicitly re-recorded at a commercial studio, but that lot of discs got lost".

Those lost discs may still exist somewhere, but the mystery of the sound of Orwell's voice will probably go on for a long time

Broadcasting Parliament.

I have spent most of my life broadcasting from Parliament, in one way or another. Perhaps the best way to round off is to look back at the way it all happened, which reflects the resistance to the BBC by politicians of all colours, and the pressures from newspapers and their proprietors, anxious not to let radio, and later television, reduce their daily sales.

Churchill's attempt

The first real attempt to put Parliament on the air came from Winston Churchill. Returning from the USA in January 1942 after the attack on Pearl Harbour, and having had a mild heart attack, Churchill asked the war cabinet if his Commons statement could be recorded through a

Chapter Ten: Ups and Downs as a Freelance

microphone, so that he could avoid the strain of making a similar broadcast outside the Commons on the same day. But the Cabinet was wary: what about possible interjections? What about requests by leaders of other parties also to have their speeches broadcast? The conclusion was unequivocal: "the broadcasting of Parliament generally was strongly deprecated". It turns out that Clement Attlee, sitting on the Ullswater committee on the renewal of the BBC's charter in 1935, had strongly opposed a BBC reporter being allowed to sit in the Gallery and broadcast an account of proceedings.

However, on his return from the USA Churchill seems to have swung the cabinet round, saying that as an experiment, an 'electrical recording' could be made of his statement, that separate motions would be required for each individual recording, and that it should be left to a free vote of the house. But so many objections were raised by MPs when the proposal was debated that Churchill said, "I do not intend to press it". He was clearly not pleased that he had to do a separate broadcast and dismissed the idea of a committee to look at the implications, replying shortly: "I think I have had enough of it". It took another 36 years before broadcasting of Parliament began in earnest.

Reith and Haley

Sir John Reith, the first Director-General of the BBC, had made several attempts in the Twenties to broadcast important Parliamentary speeches – but failed. He did succeed in establishing *The Week in Westminster*, by cleverly claiming that it was aimed at informing working-class

Chapter Ten: Ups and Downs as a Freelance

women about politics, and by inviting women MPs to give talks. It is the BBC's longest-running programme. But the BBC was denied even having a reporter in the Gallery until after the Second World War. In 1945 the new Director-General of the BBC, William Haley, decided to take matters into his own hands. In October 1945 he began *'Today in Parliament'*, based on edited news agency reports. And it was read by a newsreader, at 10.45 p.m. Initially it had audiences of around two and a half million. It was a success, and in the BBC's Licence and Agreement, part of the 1947 BBC Charter, it became a requirement. In a debate on the matter in 1946, the Labour minister Herbert Morrison said, "We thought it right to lay down in black and white that it is the duty of the BBC to keep the country informed of Parliamentary affairs". It is the only radio programme that the BBC is instructed by the government to broadcast. And it continues today, with its partner programme, *'Yesterday in Parliament'*, which I presented myself for many years, both on the staff and as a freelance.

In the late 70s, the Commons finally approved the broadcasting of debates, after many committees, discussions, and votes. The BBC did a short experiment – as they later did with TV – and once under way – from April 4th, 1978 - it allowed voice extracts in TIP and YIP*, live transmissions of important statements, and the use of 'clips'* in the news, and in programmes like *'Today'*, *The World at One'* and *'PM'*. I often did a turn as commentator for Radio 4, sitting in the cramped, glass-fronted box at the end of the Commons chamber. It was located on the government side, but it would have been far better if it had

Chapter Ten: Ups and Downs as a Freelance

been on the opposition side, as from that position we could have seen the faces of ministers at the Despatch Box when answering questions and making statements. It was from this glass box that I covered the famous Saturday morning debate on the invasion of the Falkland Isles in 1982. The move towards televising started in the Lords first, with sizeable cameras and unobtrusive cameramen having to go into the chamber during debates to work them.

Manned cameras in the House of Lords Chamber when TV broadcasting started there. The new commentary box built for our use can be seen above the clock in the Press Gallery.

It took a time before remote control cameras could be installed – as can be seen in the Commons chamber.

Chapter Ten: Ups and Downs as a Freelance

Remote control cameras in the Commons chamber, fixed under the side galleries, and controlled from Millbank.

Fighting for YIP

Editors were kind to me, and I became a regular presenter of *Yesterday in Parliament* and settled into a comfortable pattern of working. We became a close band of broadcasters, loyal, as so often in the BBC, to the programme we put together night after night. In the Parliamentary recesses, we would go out on trips to pubs along the river for a liquid lunch. And all the time the technology was changing, from ¼" magnetic tape to sound editing of video cassettes at our desks, to digital editing, which we learned as we went along.

Chapter Ten: Ups and Downs as a Freelance

In 1997 it looked as though senior managers were going to axe *YIP* after over 50 years of transmissions. I played my part in lobbying and writing articles to argue that it should be retained. Over a million people still listened to *YIP* in the morning, and it was one of the few places where the speeches of backbenchers* and peers could still be heard. Newspapers had given up employing regular staff in the Press Gallery. I pointed out that two years previously the BBC's deputy Director-General made a speech at Westminster saying the BBC reported Parliament 'willingly and with great pride'. Betty Boothroyd, the then Speaker, met the Chairman of the BBC, who was not much pleased that there were those within the BBC (who included myself) working against his plans. But in the end, it was decided to leave *YIP* alone, and it continues to this day, a fine example of public service broadcasting.

Chapter Ten: Ups and Downs as a Freelance

Playing my part

The fight to report Parliament, then to broadcast it, and also to inform the public accurately about their representatives, is a long and honourable one. I was one of many who strove to persuade our leaders, both in government, in Parliament and in the BBC, that it was worth it. I suppose I must have spent nearly forty years reporting Parliament for radio and TV, for News, special programmes, the Regions, *Nationwide*, *The World Tonight*, the Overseas Services, Obituaries and many more. I went to many seaside resorts for innumerable party conferences. I covered every election campaign from 1964 to 1992. I helped Peter Sissons with *Election Call*.

The Author assisting Peter Sissons in the studio with Election Call

I took part in several results programmes on the night. I learnt a lot about the less well-known parts of Britain by

Chapter Ten: Ups and Downs as a Freelance

making programmes about by-elections in urban and rural constituencies. And I got to know hundreds of MPs.

I hope I can say that this book gives a true account of my successes, my failures, my mis-judgements, and my minor triumphs. No politicians have been hurt in the writing of it!

INDEX

A

Adams, Tom 35

Adamson, Sir Campbell 17

Arlott, John 51

B

Barber, Anthony 69

Barker, Raymond 98

Barnes, John 63

Benn, Tony 14, 93-97

Bethell, Nicholas (Lord) 35

Betjeman, John 29

Biggs-Davison, Sir John 84

Blunt, Sir Anthony 21, 81

Bomb (Brighton) 1, 2, 23, 89

Bomb, CS Gas (Westminster) 1, 2, 68-69

Bomb (Whitehall) 69

Bonarjee, Steve 46

Booth, Albert 77

Boothroyd, Betty (Speaker) 120

Bottomley, Arthur 100

Bragg, Melvyn 42

Bridges, John 47

Brittan, Leon 32

Broadcasting of Parliament 83, 108, 115-118

Brown, George 74

Brown, Ron (Hackney South) 76

Brown, Ron (Leith) 76

Brunson, Michael 92

Budgen, Nicholas 10

Burton, Humphrey 48

Butler, David 64

C

Callaghan, James 14, 15, 73

Carvel, Robert 63

Churchill Sir Winston 9, 110, 115, 116

Churchill, Winston (Jnr) 78, 79

CDs 107-109, 111-112

Clarke, Kenneth 32

Cleverdon, Douglas 47

Cole, John 23, 89, 100

Cook, Peter 31, 33

Cook, Robin 47

Curtois, Brian 80

D

Dalyell, Tam 71

Davison, Prof. Peter 114

Davies, W.P.C. 29

Davis, Anthony 12

Day, Robin ('Poor Man's ') 68

Desborough, John 24

Dods 107

Donaldson, Peter 85

Douglas-Home, Sir Alec 2, 5, 62

E

Eggington, Andrea 7

Esslin, Martin 114

F

Falklands War 21, 83, 84, 86, 108

Faria, Reita 52

Faulds, Andrew 69

Foot, Michael 14, 77

Foster, Rodney 80

Fowler, Norman 9, 10, 32

Frost, David 9, 10, 31, 34, 40

G

General Election 1964 2, 12, 61

Gilliam, Laurence 47

Glasgow, Alex 49

Goldberg, Anatol 62

Goldby, Derek 40

Gordon, Adam 40

Griffin, Jasper 29

Grimond, Jo 99

Gummer, John 32

H

Hailsham, Lord 22, 82

Haley, Sir William 117

Hamilton, Willie 108

Harmsworth, Lord 7

Harrison, John 23, 89

Haviland, Julian 74

Healey, Denis 95-96

Heath, Edward 16-22, 65

Heffer, Eric 100

Heseltine, Michael 1, 110

Holmes, David 80, 86

Honours List 86

Hosken, John 88

Howard, Michael 32, 110

Howard, George 85

Howe, Derek 23, 90

Hoyle, Doug 83

Humphrys, John 102

Hunt, Norman 61-62

Hutton, Sir Len 26

I

Ingham, Bernard 24

Israel 36-38, 41, 133

J

James, P.D. (Baroness) 102

Jenkins, Roy 65, 66, 68, 75, 83, 100

Jones, Christopher 65, 80

Jones, Colonel 'H' 86

K

Khashoggi, Soraya 79

Khruschev, Nikita 62

King, Horace 69

Kinnock, Neil 91, 92, 94

L

Lamont, Norman 32

Lang, Ian 43, 44

Leadbitter, Ted 82

Leeson, Nick 34

Le Fanu, Sir Victor (Sergeant-at-Arms) 21

Lewis, Noel 82

Lobby, The 22, 24, 50, 76, 77, 87, 95

'Love and Hate' 104

M

Macmillan, Harold 9, 10

Mackay, Sgt Ian 86

Magee, Patrick 89

Major, John 2, 8, 7, 100

Mallalieu, Sir Lance 28

Mansfield, Jayne 53

Mansell, Gerard 60

Margach, James 18

Martin, David 57

Mayhew, Lord 84

McKenzie, Robert 46

Mellor, David 82

MEPs 3, 42, 103, 105, 106

Merriman, Eric 47

Mills, Roger 51

Mintoff, Dom 72

Moir, Guthrie 40

Moncrieff, Chris 78

Montgomery, F.M. of Alamein 30

Morrison, Herbert 117

Mosley, Sir Oswald 32

Moyle, Douglas 114

Mullin, Chris 93, 94

Muncaster, Martin 49

N

Nabarro, Sir Gerald 67

Neave, Airey 1, 72

News on Line 3, 105-107

O

Obituaries 98-100, 121

O'Grady, Dorothy 55-59

Orwell, George (Eric Blair) 113-115

P

Paisley, Rev. Ian 111

Parker, Bruce 53

Patten, Chris 100

Powell, Enoch 50

Protheroe, Alan 85

R

Rayner, Ted 16, 65

Reid, Bob 62

Reagan, President Ronald 88

Rees, Peter 73

Reith, Sir John 116

Robbins, Peter 83

Roth, Andrew 104

Rozhdestvenskii, Gennadi 48

S

Sandys, Duncan 15

Scott, Peter Hardiman 15, 80

Semprini, Albert 46

Shah, Samir 7

Shanks, Michael 61

Silkin, John 96

Sissons, Peter 121

Sloman, Ann 63

Smith, John 99

Snagge, John 47, 48

Snow, John 29

Sound Recording 111, 112

Springfield, Dusty 44

Stern, Geoffrey 61

Stonehouse, John 98

T

Temple-Morris, Peter 9

Tennyson, Hallam 60

Thatcher, Denis 22, 23, 95

Thatcher, Margaret 1, 2, 17, 18, 21-24, 64, 72, 73, 79, 81, 82, 89, 108

Thomas, George (Speaker) 71

Trenchard, Lord 84

Trethowan, Sir Ian 43

Trueman, Fred 26, 27, 33

Tusa, John 43, 62

V

Varley, Eric 93

Viggers, Peter 32

Voss Bark, Conrad 65, 80

W

Wall, Sir Patrick 85

Weatherill, Jack (Speaker) 96, 97, 108

Wheldon, Huw 42, 48

Whitehead, Phillip 42, 94, 95

Whitelaw, Willie 1, 90, 91

Whitney, Ray 84

Wilde, Jimmy 26

Williams, Sir Tom 82

Williamson, Harold 49

Wilson, Harold 2, 11, 12, 14, 22, 62, 65, 99

Wilson, John 63

Windlesham, Lord 40

Woodcock, George 27

Woon, Peter 43

Wyndham Goldie, Grace 5

Y

Yesterday in Parliament (YIP) 3, 102, 117, 119, 120

Glossary

Adjournment: The end of the day's business, usually preceded by a half-hour debate on an issue raised by a backbench MP.

Attachment: A period of time, often three months, working for another BBC department or section from one's own, to learn different skills, or to practise them.

Autocue: A system where one's script rolls up in front of the camera lens, in fact appearing on a piece of glass set at 45 degrees to the lens. In the big studios there were autocue assistants who ran the script machines for you. At Westminster in the self-operated studio, we typed our scripts on acetate, fed them into a machine beside the desk, set our reading speed on it, and then when cued (given the green light to begin) we controlled the running of the script with a foot pedal below the desk.

Backbenchers: Those who sit behind the government, or the Labour front bench, and who have no official role. Select Committees are formed from backbenchers on both sides of the House. And large parties have specialised committees monitoring different departments.

Blair: Eric Blair was George Orwell's real name.

By-Election: An election which takes place between general elections, in a single constituency, when the sitting MP resigns or dies, leaving the seat vacant. Now and then there is a delay of several months before the by-election is held. And sometimes several by-elections are held on the same day (usually to allay bad news).

Charter Renewal: The BBC's Royal Charter has to be reviewed every 10 years, making it subject to government scrutiny and the pressures of MPs. The next Charter Review, which includes the question of whether to continue the system of funding through the licence fee, is in 2027. The current BBC Chairman has called for such reviews to end.

Clip: A short extract of a speech, either for radio or later for television, inserted into a news report by a correspondent.

Commons Fees Office: Originally it paid MPs' expenses, but after the scandal, was abolished in 2010, and responsibility was transferred to the Independent Parliamentary Standards Authority (IPSA), which is overseen by a Speaker's Committee.

Conscription: Compulsory throughout the 50s in England, Wales and Scotland (but not Northern Ireland) for all boys over 18, requiring two years in either the Army, the Navy or the Air Force. Very few were called up into the Navy.

Crew: Usually a cameraman and a sound man. Sometimes a lighting man as well.

Commentary Box: Screened-off section at the far-end of the Commons Chamber with about four seats for BBC and other commentators, accessed through the Members' Lobby, locked during a vote.

Despatch Boxes: In the Commons, there is a Despatch Box on either side of the main table, from which ministers and shadow ministers speak.

EMI: A large music and record producer with studios at Abbey Road in North London: now owned by Sony Music Publishing.

Film: In my day, working for news, the film was often 16mm, shot in black and white, and had to be processed when we returned to the studios. To make the 6pm deadline, we often had to edit it in negative (black on white) and then write a script to fit, in the very little time left before live transmission at 6pm, or 6.20.

Freelance: Working for the BBC for a fee, but not on the salaried staff.

Goy: Hebrew, and Yiddish, for non-Jew. Can be pejorative.

Guillotine: A parliamentary motion to cut short debate on a bill, by subjecting it to a timetable. This often happens when governments lose patience with the opposition's delaying tactics.

Hodder: A large publishing group with a Spoken Word section (for CDs and Kindle) later taken over by Headline, by W.H.Smith, and then in 2004 by Hachette Ltd.

Kibbutz: A communal settlement in Israel, usually agricultural, where most things are shared.

The Lobby: The square Hall just outside the Commons chamber, to which political correspondents of the press and radio and television are admitted, to mix with MPs. Hence they are also called 'Lobby Correspondents' and collectively, 'The Lobby'. They have their own rules of behaviour, not always followed.

Lip mike: A microphone held close to one's upper lip, to restrict the sound of one's voice

Minister of State: A minister, not in the Cabinet, one below a Secretary of State.

MP3: A compressed file which takes up much less space than a CD.

Pager: Before the era of cellphones, duty reporters were issued with this gadget which fitted on one's belt, and when the newsroom wanted you, especially at weekends and during the night they 'beeped' you, and you rang in to ask what the problem was.

Point of Order: When an MP raises a question of procedure, rather than the substance of a bill or a motion.

Press Association: The main news agency, also known as the PA.

Press Gallery, or 'the Gallery': Where newspaper reporters, news agencies and sketchwriters used to sit. In the gallery above the Speaker. Opposite is the screened-off public gallery.

Public Domain: A document is in the public domain if it has been officially published. It is available to the public and not subject to copyright laws.

Purchase tax: A tax on luxury goods, abolished in 1973, replaced by VAT when we joined the Common Market.

Select Committee: A committee set up to monitor a government department, or for a special purpose. The membership, comprising MPs elected by their own party, is balanced between the parties, usually with a govt majority. Chairmen are paid extra.

SPADs: Special advisers to ministers; they are political, but when appointed become temporary civil servants.

Tribune Group: Consists of Labour MPs on the Centre Left.

Voice Feed: A live input into a programme from an outside source, such as a reporter at an election count.

Vote: A vote in the Commons usually takes about 15 minutes, as MPs have to 'divide' and be counted by the whips going through separate voting lobbies. No business is conducted in the Chamber during a vote.

Whip: One of about a dozen junior members of the government who control and enforce Parliamentary business. They also each have a regional duty of keeping in touch with their local members. They do not speak in the House or give interviews. They are not supposed to write books, although the Tory Chief Whip Simon Hart has recently done so. They can recommend backbenchers for promotion, or for overseas trips, and they can also block their progress. The Chief Whip attends Cabinet. A 'whip' is also a weekly advice note about upcoming votes. 'Three-line whips' are mandatory. The Opposition also has Whips. Each side also has a 'Pairing Whip' who agrees with his opposite number to let MPs miss votes, provided a government majority is maintained. Only on a 'free vote' can an MP exercise his or her conscience.

Woolsack: Where by tradition the Lord Speaker of the House of Lords sits.

YIP and TIP: *Yesterday in Parliament* and *Today in Parliament*

YMCA: Young Men's Christian Association

Photos and Sources

1. The author: Own photo.

1 AMONG THE PREMIERS

2. Douglas-Home:
   https://en.wikipedia.org/wiki/Alec_Douglas-Home
3. Major:
   https://en.wikipedia.org/wiki/John_Major#/media/File:John_Major_1993_(3).jpg
4. Macmillan:
   https://www.britannica.com/biography/Harold-Macmillan
5. Wilson: https://simple.wikipedia.org/wiki/Harold_Wilson
6. Author with Harold Wilson from *"Television – Here is the News"* by Anthony Davis
7. Callaghan: https://en.wikipedia.org/wiki/James_Callaghan Attribution: © European Communities, 1975
8. Heath: https://www.theoldie.co.uk/blog/memory-lane-feeding-time-at-the-zoo-with-ted-heath (Accompanied an article the author wrote for The Oldie)
9. Thatcher:
   https://en.wikipedia.org/wiki/Margaret_Thatcher#/media/File:Margaret_Thatcher_(1983).jpg/2 ©the Thatcher Estate
10. Parliamentary Lobby Centenary Lunch: Author's own.

2. GETTING THERE

11. Woodcock
    https://en.wikipedia.org/wiki/George_Woodcock_(trade_unionist)

12. Monty:
https://en.wikipedia.org/wiki/Bernard_Montgomery
13. Mosley: https://en.wikipedia.org/wiki/Oswald_Mosley
14. Frost:
https://simple.wikipedia.org/wiki/David_Frost#/media/File:David_Frost_Rumsfeld_interview_cropped.jpg
15. Adams:
https://en.wikipedia.org/wiki/Tom_Adams_(politician)

3. JOINING THE BBC

16. Esslin: https://www.bbc.co.uk/programmes/p07sxdq8
17. Whitehead:
https://en.wikipedia.org/wiki/Phillip_Whitehead under https://creativecommons.org/licenses/by-sa/3.0/ ©John Whitby
18. Dusty: https://en.wikipedia.org/wiki/Dusty_Springfield

4. GETTING AROUND

19. Semprini: https://en.wikipedia.org/wiki/Alberto_Semprini
20. Snagge: https://en.wikipedia.org/wiki/John_Snagge
21. Powell: https://en.wikipedia.org/wiki/Enoch_Powell https://creativecommons.org/licenses/by-sa/3.0/ ©Allan Warren
22. Arlott: https://en.wikipedia.org/wiki/John_Arlott (at BBC c.1952)
23. Faria: https://en.wikipedia.org/wiki/Reita_Faria https://creativecommons.org/licenses/by-sa/2.0/ Frederick Noronha
24. Mansfield:
https://en.wikipedia.org/wiki/Jayne_Mansfield#/media/File:ETH-Bibliothek_Z%C3%BCrich,_Bildarchiv_-_Com_C06-137-003_-_Jayne_Mansfield_(1).jpg

https://creativecommons.org/licenses/by/4.0/
ETH-Bibliothek Zürich, Bildarchiv / Fotograf: Comet Photo AG (Zürich)

5. MRS O'GRADY

25. O'Grady: source not found

6. FINDING A JOB

26. Mansell: https://www.bbc.co.uk/programmes/p06cf1jx

7. TO THE COMMONS

27. Nabarro: https://en.wikipedia.org/wiki/Gerald_Nabarro
©Rex Coleman, for Baron Studios
28. Dalyell: https://en.wikipedia.org/wiki/Tam_Dalyell Open Media Ltd https://creativecommons.org/licenses/by-sa/3.0/
29. Neave: https://www.beaconsfieldhistory.org.uk/content/beaconsfield-history/people/airey-neave-2
30. George Brown: https://en.wikipedia.org/wiki/George_Brown,_Baron_George-Brown
31. Ron Brown (Hackney South and Shoreditch): Copied by me from Times Guide to the House of Commons 1974
32. Ron Brown (Leith): Copied by me from Times Guide to the House of Commons 1987
33. BBC Parliamentary Team: Author's

8. THATCHER IN NO.10

34. Blunt: https://en.wikipedia.org/wiki/Anthony_Blunt
35. H. Jones: https://en.wikipedia.org/wiki/H._Jones

36. Reagan: https://en.wikipedia.org/wiki/Ronald_Reagan
37. Mrs Thatcher:
https://en.wikipedia.org/wiki/Margaret_Thatcher#/media/File:Margaret_Thatcher_(1983).jpg/2
38. Willie Whitelaw:
https://www.azquotes.com/author/41225-William_Whitelaw_1st_Viscount_Whitelaw
39. Kinnock: https://en.wikipedia.org/wiki/Neil_Kinnock
Raymond Reuter, © European Communities, 1995
https://creativecommons.org/licenses/by/4.0/

9. PROBLEMS WITH BENN

40. Benn: https://en.wikipedia.org/wiki/Tony_Benn
Isujosh https://creativecommons.org/licenses/by-sa/3.0/
41. Healey: https://en.wikipedia.org/wiki/Denis_Healey
42. Grimond: https://en.wikipedia.org/wiki/Jo_Grimond

10. UPS AND DOWNS

43. Great Parliamentary Speeches CD: Author's.
44. Great Political Speeches CD: Author's
45. Paisley: https://en.wikipedia.org/wiki/Ian_Paisley @ European Union, 1998 - 2025
46. Orwell: https://en.wikipedia.org/wiki/George_Orwell
47. Churchill:
https://commons.wikimedia.org/wiki/File:Winston_Churchill_at_a_BBC_microphone_about_to_broadcast_to_the_nation_on_the_afternoon_of_VE_Day,_8_May_1945._H41843.jpg
48. House of Lords camera
49. House of Commons remote control cameras

50. Boothroyd:
> https://en.wikipedia.org/wiki/Betty_Boothroyd
> https://api.parliament.uk/Live/photo/JBXhBMhD.jpeg?download=true https://creativecommons.org/licenses/by/3.0/

51. Author with Peter Sissons: Author's

11. COVER

52. Author Outside Parliament: Author's

Printed in Dunstable, United Kingdom